Basic cooking

All you need to cook really well in no time at all

Sabine Sälzer   Sebastian Dickhaut

BARNES & NOBLE

NEW YORK

Sebastian Dickhaut...

lives in Munich where he writes books
and magazine articles on food and drink.
He is a regular contributor to several food
magazines. Sebastian helped develop the
concept of the Basics book series and wrote
the text for this as for other Basics books.

Sabine Sälzer...

writes cookbooks, quite by accident but
with great passion. She's not always very
patient but always full of enthusiasm.
She loves lemons, because they improve
nearly everything, and full fridges so she
always buys too much. And she helped
develop the Basics concept and wrote the
recipes for this book.

© 2004 by GRÄFE UND UNZER VERLAG
GmbH, Munich

This 2006 edition published by Barnes &
Noble, Inc. by arrangement with GRÄFE
UND UNZER VERLAG GmbH, Munich

Picture credits:

Barbara Bonisolli: recipes, steps, cooking
methods, "quick 17" and "fantastic 14",
fish p102.

Axel Walter: all people photography;
still life opener p7.

Peter von Felbert: insets on pp63, 82, 83,
113.

StockFood:
Walter Pfisterer: pasta pp38 and 40;
Picture Box: onion pp66 and 116
Maximilian Stock: tomato cover, pp132 and
135; egg pp 10, 84, 86; fish p100; apple p151
Gerhard Bumann: carrot p135
S. & P. Eising: cream p148
Michael Boyny: p168 top

Production:

bookwise Medienproduktion GmbH,
Munich

This edition translated and typeset by
Silva Editions Ltd, Purley

Translators: Sylvia Goulding, Brigitta Pauley,
Rafael Pauley, Katherine Taylor
American editor: Adèle Linderholm
Index: Mike Goulding

ISBN-13: 978-0-7607-8439-6
ISBN-10: 0-7607-8439-6

Printed and bound in China

1 3 5 7 9 10 8 6 4 2

Basic cooking
Contents

Know How

To simply cook
no more, no less

Basics are the white T-shirt and the neat black skirt. The exquisite Italian shoes and the fabulous boutique scarf. And, of course, great-uncle's Tuxedo. Classics, really. Even if I'd much prefer to wear something warm or something fashionable to show off.

Wait a minute, isn't this a cookbook? Of course. Bruschetta with tomatoes and spaghetti with lemon cream, granny's roast pork and Frank's chocolate mousse, fiery mojo from Spain and homemade mayonnaise—all Basics. Everything that always fits and is in fashion—but not without your own personal touch.

We wanted to write a cookbook. Yes, yet another one! Not a bible, not a dictionary, not a coffee table book. Not one thousand recipes. Not two thousand variations. Just one hundred favorite dishes—Basic recipes, which can lead you to a million ideas. Stupid ideas are also tolerated, but not too many, please.

It did become a cookbook in the end—for a kitchen full of starving friends as well as for you alone on your desert island. A book that states that eating is vital, but that it must not always be taken too seriously. Just keep on reading and you'll be there in no time. Be Basic. Nothing extra, nothing important missing.

"Eating is fun!"
We know that.
"So is food shopping."
Really?

Why should we be worse off than the people on TV? Dancing through lofts with our morning coffee, happily putting a soufflé in the oven at lunchtime, laughing with friends around a table at night. Sounds great! But there's a hitch: We have to go shopping first. And so far we've never seen anyone on TV do that (except in the ads).

They never show anyone who chases down aisles, fights his/her way to the salad counter, or first looks at the price of a bottle of wine before looking at the wine itself. But that's what we do nearly every single day. And it can get quite hectic. But it can also be done in quite a relaxed way.

Sure, pleasure really only comes with eating. But we can allow ourselves some "prepleasure" at the supermarket. If we go about it cleverly—and if we follow the three basic rules of smart shopping:

I know something. I plan something. And now I do it!

Smart shopping

75 percent of us—(Americans!) don't know in the afternoon what we're going to have for dinner. Smart?

Going shopping can sometimes do you good. Picking whatever you feel like and maybe even discovering something you'll love forever, that's not bad! But if you have to buy your food while you are on a shopping expedition, then you'll get fed up with it very quickly. Because the following day only the wrong stuff will be in the fridge. Because everything's so expensive. It's much smarter if you start by saying:

"I know something"

Sounds almost like at school. But this time it has to do with your own kitchen. If you know that you have a bell pepper, yesterday's rice, and a bottle of soy sauce somewhere, maybe an idea for dinner will spring to mind. And if you happen to know a good place to buy fish, it is no problem for you to create a wonderful rice dish—just like that.

An expert in the art of living always has a few Basic bits at home—and can make a good meal out of them. They will be presented on the next pages. Together with our recipes and half an hour's food shopping, they provide everything for a culinary feast.

To produce something good without getting into a state also means knowing what's good. A question of money? A matter of taste? All right. But then, we at least want to know what's not good. Hard lentils are not good. That's when a can of cooked lentils, which can be spiced up with a dash of balsamic vinegar, comes in handy. Tough meat isn't good either. And if you're the kind of person who chews on his/her cheap pork chops for ages and then finally still ends up phoning for a pizza, you'll be better off next time buying good organic meat in the first place. Even financially.

Seasonal food is good. Apples early in season are neither cheap nor tasty. For practical reasons: Fruit and vegetables in season not only taste better, but are also much cheaper, because so much of it is around. Especially when it has been grown locally and not flown and driven for miles and miles. After having been harvested much too early. And that is also good for our green conscience.

"I plan something"

75 percent of us—(Americans!)—don't know in the afternoon what we're going to have for dinner. We often end up in a fast-food restaurant or with takeout. Just because we can't think of anything else to do to still our hunger. Somehow, not brilliant, nor creative.

In that case, I'd rather plan a little ahead. In the old days, a menu was written a week in advance. Nowadays you just need to scribble down the food you want to eat that day. A shopping list will do the trick. It can be on the reverse side of your last receipt or a page in your special shopping book. The main thing is that it'll make it to the checkout. And not stay on the kitchen table.

Smart shoppers organize their work: One corner of the list is for the butcher, one for the grocer, one for the supermarket. Or if it's only to be the supermarket, then one corner is for the grocery section, one for the fruit department, and one for the cheese counter. You know the layout of your store.

"And now I do it!"

That means: Go out and get it! And if I come across something that suits me better or is cheaper than what I planned to buy: I'll take it anyway! As a real Basics cook, I'm an expert, I know something, I've thought of something. And I also enjoy the luxury of completely ignoring all of that! After all, I know the most important ground rules and I enjoy playing around with them.

Three golden rules
for shopping

1 Eat well beforehand
If you go hungry to the supermarket, you'll buy everything just to fill yourself up. Too expensive. However: If you eat until you drop, you won't feel like thinking about food and you'll try to get out of there as soon as possible. No good either because:

2 Take time, but don't waste time
Avoid last-minute shopping, because you will grab the first thing you see. And this is often too expensive. When shopping leisurely, more items will land in your basket for the same price. Therefore concentrate on shopping and:

3 Look there, down below
Right shelf, at eye level—1 pound coffee for $5.99. Please bend down—1 pound for $5.25. Now turn to the left—ah, there's the flour. It's arranged so that where you look first is the most expensive place. It gets cheaper when you look again. And what you actually want, you'll only find after a long search. So be careful, or your basket will be full of unwanted stuff at maximum price.

Think big
Unfortunately, singles know what we're talking about: The smaller the package, the more expensive it is. Hardly any difference really whether you buy a big or a small package of crackers. And loose foods are often cheaper than prepacked ones.

Cool Basics

"Dear Basics, it's quite chilly in here, but I must say your food's keeping well. Kind regards, your fridge."

What do raisins and pickles have in common? They don't need to be in the fridge. Because they have been preserved in a smart way, invented by smart people a long time ago, before the time of fridges. They weren't bad times we think, while nibbling our delicious marinated olives. But it's good that they're over because otherwise the beer we have with it would be warm.

Nowadays, a kitchen without cupboards is more acceptable than a household without chilling supplied via a socket. Because there is always something "freeze fanatics" can find and discover. Climatic conditions range from average winter temperatures in the fridge to arctic conditions in the freezer. And some foods even enjoy spring temperatures.

Climate research in the fridge

In an average fridge, temperatures range from 32 to 49 °F. The same rule applies to mini bars with an ice compartment and to luxury coolers with a champagne compartment: It's always cooler at the back and bottom than in front and above. It's therefore best to put fish on the bottom shelf and push it as far back as possible.

Exceptions? There are three: When the ice compartment is at the top, it's colder directly underneath. And it's much warmer in the chiller drawers at the bottom of the fridge, because the shelf right above prevents the cold air from descending. And: There's a moderate climate in the fridge door that becomes even more moderate, i.e. warmer, each time you open it. Now to the ice compartment: The basic model will cool down to 32 °F, and is therefore only suitable for ice cubes. If fat or sugar is added to foods, their freezing point sinks.

Arctic conditions in the freezer

You will find temperatures of -4 °F and lower in freezers, a bitter cold, in which you wouldn't feel like moving. And that's why life in a freezer goes into slow motion, which means food keeps longer in it. But that doesn't mean it has an eternal life. Air and water continue to do their jobs, although slowed down. The slow aging of foods in their cold sleep can be slowed down even more by packing them properly—meaning in a way that is airtight. You can see what happens if this is not the case: A half-open deep-frozen french fries bag contains a few dried-up fries and a lot of ice. It's often said that frozen vegetables contain more nutrients than fresh. This is only true as long as the frozen goods have not stayed in their arctic compartments for months—or even years—on end. Otherwise it's better fresh. Sure, frozen peas or puff pastry make our life really easy and a freezer is the ideal home for leftover soup. But: Fresh fish filets or a tender steak are not necessarily Basics for the freezer stock—they should be thrown directly into the pan.

Some like it fresh

Being children of the sun, many kinds of fruit and veg don't like fridge temperatures at all. Some cannot stand the cold: Bananas for instance. Some lose their flavor forever, such as tomatoes; others don't like long cold periods, but are really refreshing after a short chilling period just before consumption—melons for example.

Danger alert!

- Don't buy rusty, dented, or bulging cans.
- Make sure carton eggs are clean and not cracked.
- Choose frozen items last; carry them home in separate bags to avoid contamination "by drip."
- Refrigerate perishables as soon as you are home.
- Check often that the fridge temperature does not go above 40 °F and the freezer temperature above 0 °F.
- Make sure air can circulate in the freezer.
- Don't store potatoes, onions etc. under the sink where leaks may damage them.
- Food and cleaning supplies are not happy bedfellows.

The Basic chilled stock: How to keep what, where, and how long

Top and middle

Cheese for sandwiches and "au gratin" (e.g. cheddar), for grating (e.g. Parmesan), for nibbling (e.g. Swiss, blue cheese, or soft cheese), and cream cheese, mozzarella, or others
How: in an airtight container, wrapped in aluminum foil or covered with paper or a damp cloth. Keep strong cheeses separate; cream cheese or mozzarella in its own packaging
How long: depending on the kind of cheese, 3 days to 2 weeks or use-by date

Milk, cream, yogurt, crème fraîche, buttermilk, sour cream, mascarpone
How: store in the middle rather than at the top; close well after opening; always use a clean spoon
How long: until use-by date; after opening 2–5 days

Bottom or coldest place

Meat, cold cuts, fish
How: meat and fish without wrapping on a plate or in a dish, covered, but not quite airtight; poultry kept separate; cold cuts without wrapping, separated, and in as few layers as possible in an airtight container; smoked products separate
How long: ground meat maximum 1 day, poultry and chopped meat 1–2 days, other meat 2–3 days, cooked meat 3 days; fish, fresh 1–2 days, smoked, pickled, marinated after opening 2–3 days, cooked 2–3 days; cold cuts 2–4 days, smoked produce 1 week or more

Door

Butter, eggs, opened cans, opened drinks
How: in respective compartments
How long: butter and eggs until use-by date

Chiller drawers

Vegetables such as scallions, leeks, carrots, cabbages, and beets are Basics, salads like Chinese cabbage, romaine lettuce, or chicory keep longer; mushrooms and soup vegetables you should have—just in case; otherwise according to season and you own personal taste
How: loose, delicate vegetables not quite airtight in foil or damp cloth;
How long: leaf vegetables and mushrooms 2–3 days, root vegetables such as carrots or beets 1–2 weeks, the rest 1 week

Herbs such as basil, parsley, and chives are always good; dill, tarragon, chervil, cress, oregano, rosemary, sage, thyme for specials
How: wrapped in foil or a damp cloth
How long: delicate ones 2–3 days, others 4–7 days

Fresh berries
How: separated from other fruit, berries should not be too close to one another, in single layers covered with a damp cloth
How long: 1–3 days

The freezer

Peas, spinach, chopped herbs; french fries, puff pastry, ready-baked products (toast, French bread etc.), frozen fish filets, shrimp, frozen berries, ice cream, ice cubes; homecooked food, ready-made meals for emergencies
How: in airtight containers and freezer bags (reseal already opened food stuffs)
How long: frozen products until use-by date, after defrosting like fresh products; bread and cake 1–3 months; fish 3–6 months; fruit and veg 6 months (e.g. berries) to 12 months (e.g. carrots); meat 6 months (poultry, pork) to 12 months (lamb, beef); home-cooked dishes 3–6 months

Outside

Eggplant, cucumbers, potatoes, garlic, peppers, tomatoes, zucchini, onions; apples, bananas, kiwis, citrus fruit, and other exotic fruit
How: in the dark (unless for ripening in storage), airy and dry. Potatoes, onions, garlic 43–59 °F, veg 50–59 °F, fruit 54–65 °F. Fruit and veg can mutually accelerate ripening (apples kept with potatoes, pears, bananas; citrus fruit with avocados, apples, and bananas), therefore store separately
How long: according to temperature a few days (fruit), 1 week (veg), or 2 weeks (potatoes etc.)

Basics
in stock

"There is nothing to eat!" "But the fridge is full!"

Just imagine: a luxury cruise with its sumptuous buffet. Suddenly a big bang, and hours later you end up stranded on the well-known desert island — starving. Luckily, the onboard kitchen was also washed ashore, and the palm tree in front of you even has a suitable socket. But bad luck, all the provisions have sunk to the bottom of the sea. Better forget about eating as much as you like! "Not at all," a small voice whispers. A mermaid! "You can wish for three ingredients. But do think about it carefully. Be Basic!" First of all pasta, of course. Or maybe bread? "Have flour," whispers the fairy. Yes, exactly, and salt of course! "Tsk, tsk, tsk," the little fairy shakes her head towards the sea water. "What about garlic?" Of course! But butter, butter is a must. "With this heat?" Oil? "Finally, you've got it. Take care for now." Stop, don't you want something to eat? Spaghetti aglio e olio? "OK, but I'll get the wine."

From M to XL — the Basic stock for just about anybody

Be Basic — not that easy when it's for the eternal stock. What? Stock? Eternal? Isn't that a bit old-fashioned now that you can buy enough for an entire candlelit dinner right at a gas station? It can be convenient from time to time, but in the long run gas romance or daily trips to the supermarket lose their appeal.

Lazybones and other connoisseurs make up their own little Basic stock, depending on their degree of hunger. What's important: How often am I at home for a meal and who with? Is it just the little fairy or, more often, all my buddies from the office? And what about personal taste? We'll come to that later.

For a start, we recommend a stock size M for "must have": everything you need to survive in a normal household. On top of that comes size L for "likes and lusts": everything that will spice up your life. For that special extra luxury we offer size XL for "extremely luscious": all the other food we like, even if there is no other person on the planet who shares our taste.

Lots of good stuff in stock

"The kitchen is the worst place for storing food." True, with all its steam, smells, and changing temperatures, it cannot be the best place for storing food. Still, nearly everybody does it. Because it's handy. How about the basement? Too far. The larder? What's that? The cool bedroom? Who wants to sleep on peas?

Nearly everything that does not come from the refrigerated counters will survive in the kitchen for a while. Provided things are stored in dry (sealable containers), not-too-hot (far away from the stove), and particularly dark places (behind storage walls or closed doors).

Use by...

Manufacturers guarantee that their products remain practically unchanged until the use-by date. Often they're quite OK even after that date — but it could be possible that the stock cubes won't dissolve as quickly, for example. Remember: The shorter the preservation time, the shorter the extension to the expiry date.

Everything you need for a truly enjoyable survival, how to store it and how long it keeps fresh

Use-by date
Keeps until…: as long as it tastes good
Keeps almost forever: is quite okay even after one year

M for "must have"

Sugar, salt
Keep almost forever, if stored well

Wheat flour, rice, starch
Keep 1 year in a dark place, if sealed and aired, wholemeal flour keeps less long

Semolina, breadcrumbs
The same as flour, but keep only 8 months

Oat flakes, muesli
Keep 6 months, if stored airtight in the dark

Pasta
Store in the dark. Dried pasta keeps 1–2 years

Dried pulses
Keep almost forever, stored dark, dry and airy

Toast
Keeps until use-by date, opened 1 week

Pasteurized milk
Keeps until use-by date, opened and refrigerated 3–5 days

Coffee
Keeps until use-by date, opened 1–2 months, if kept airtight in a dark place

Curry, nutmeg, paprika, pepper, cinnamon
Store in the dark. Ground okay for 1 year

Dried herbs
Keep 6 months in a dark, dry place

Ready-made stock and sauces
Keep forever as powder. Cubes 6–8 months

Neutral vegetable oil
Keeps 1 year in the dark, opened less long

Regular vinegar
Keeps forever in the dark, depends on variety

Tomato purée, ketchup, mustard
Keep until use-by date, opened and refrigerated several weeks

Soy sauce
Keeps nearly 1 year, if stored in the dark

Pesto
Keeps until use-by date, opened and refrigerated a good month (covered with oil)

Capers, olives
Keep until use-by date, opened several weeks

Gherkins, pickles
Keep until use-by date, opened and refrigerated 2 weeks

Canned tomatoes
Keep until use-by date and longer, opened and refrigerated 1 week

Tuna, beans
Keep until use-by date, opened and refrigerated 2-3 days

Fruit in cans and jars, jam
Keep until use-by date, opened and refrigerated 1-2 weeks

Honey
Keeps almost forever in the dark. Crystallizes after a while

Raisins
Keep 1 year in a dry, dark place

Chocolate, cocoa powder
Keep until use-by date and longer

Almonds, hazelnuts
Keep 6 months in a dry dark place

Custard powder
Keeps until use-by date and longer

Vanilla sugar
Keeps almost forever, the aroma lasts 1 year

Baking powder
Keeps until use-by date and longer

Wine
Store in a dark, cool place. Keeps 1 year, possibly forever. Opened 1 day to 1 week

Bread
Stored in an airy, dry, dark place it keeps 2–10 days, depending on the variety

Potatoes, onions
Keep 2–3 weeks, if stored in an airy, dry, dark, not too warm place

Garlic
Same as potatoes, dried even longer

L for "likes & lusts"

Risotto rice
Keeps 1 year airtight in a dark place (air often)

Corn flakes
Keep until use-by date, opened 1–2 weeks

Crisp bread, cookies
Keep until use-by date, opened and airtight 1-2 weeks

Espresso
Keeps until use-by date, opened 1–2 months

Dried chilies, caraway seeds, cloves, juniper berries, cayenne pepper, ground ginger, dried marjoram
Keep 1 year, stored dark and dry

Oil, special, e.g. olive oil
Keeps 6–12 months in the dark, depending on variety, open a little less long

Vinegar, special (balsamic)
Keeps 6–12 months in the dark, depending on variety

Tabasco, Worcestershire sauce, other aromatic sauces
Keep almost forever in the dark

Horseradish in jars, anchovy paste, anchovies in oil
Keep until use-by date, opened and refrigerated several weeks

Mixed pickles, pepperoni, red cabbage, sun-dried tomatoes
Keep until use-by date, opened and refrigerated 2 weeks

Potted shrimps
Keep until use-by date, opened and refrigerated 2–3 days

Canned sweet corn
Same as shrimps

Dry yeast
Keeps until use-by date

XL for "extremely luscious"

Polenta
Airtight in a dark place (air often) 6–8 months

Fennel seeds
Keep 1 year, stored dark and dry

Mango chutney
Keeps until use-by date, opened and refrigerated several weeks

Coconut milk
Keeps until use-by date, opened and refrigerated 1 week

Pumpkin seeds, pine kernels
Keep 6 months in a dark and dry place

Dried mushrooms
Keep almost forever in a dark and dry place

bacon

shrimp

cheese

stock

lemon

garlic

canned tomatoes

soy sauce

pesto

balsamic vinegar

curry

capers

toast

the quick
17
Basics
for the
ultimate kick

parsley

honey

chocolate

mustard

bacon

French: lard; Italian: lardo; Spanish: beicon
It comes from the pig's belly and it is cured and smoked. Good bacon is firm, not too fat, and tastes of meat, of smoke, and only last of salt.
I d e a s : crispy bacon in salads • toss pasta in fried bacon • fry bacon, add some wine = great sauce • a slice of bacon on a turkey scallop, coated in breadcrumbs • wrap a chicken breast in bacon and fry • line an ovenproof dish with bacon • wrap liver, prunes, or cheese in bacon and cook in the oven—great tapas!

shrimp

French: crevettes; Italian: gamberetti; Spanish: gamba
Shrimp are well-known animals and have many names. Here we talk about the common cocktail shrimp, cooked and peeled. Fresh, they are only found in the sea, frozen shrimp are a good alternative. If they taste pleasantly of the sea and don't have a dark intestine, they are OK. They should be cooked gently, and only briefly.
I d e a s : potato salad/fried potatoes with shrimp • salad with shrimp and croutons, fried in garlic oil • bruschetta with shrimp, tomatoes, pesto • shrimp in scrambled eggs • spaghetti with shrimp • veal steak with fried shrimp • shrimp butter

cheese

French: fromage; Italian: formaggio; Spanish: queso
Its base is milk, but it can be cow's, buffalo's, goat's, or sheep's milk. And what it turns into can be as bland as cream cheese or as exquisite as blue cheese, creamy soft or firm and hard, mild or strong. Cheese is good for everything—provided it is good, relatively natural cheese.
I d e a s : salad dressing with feta cheese • vegetable gratin with cottage cheese • toasted bread with baked camembert • cheese sauce with cooked meat • grated Parmesan with spinach or carrots • grated Swiss cheese in vegetable soup • fried eggs with grated cheese • mozzarella with caramelized fruit as dessert

stock

French: fond, bouillon; Italian: brodo; Spanish: caldo
Whether it's beef, chicken, fish, or vegetable stock—every Basic cook should have a favorite stock in the house. Ideally, you should keep homemade stock in your freezer, in containers or as cubes. But pastes, cubes, or powders also have a soothing effect on body and soul. Basic recipes for stock: pages 66, 78, 80, 82
I d e a s : improve a vinaigrette with stock • stew potatoes in stock • cook pasta for salads in stock • instead of adding cream to soups and sauces, add a little stock • use stock instead of water for sauces • stock with croutons and onions • chicken stock with lemon, very refreshing

lemon

French: citron; Italian: limone; Spanish: limón
Very Basic: available throughout the world and at your local store. Suitable for cooking, baking, mixing, decorating, and even when doing the dishes. Its juice is refreshing and adds flavor. The—organic (!)—zest gives desserts an interesting taste and texture and jazzes up most sauces.
I d e a s : lemon in salad, stimulating • lemon juice improves soups and sauces • lemon zest in stew • briefly cooked lemon slices with fish • caramelize sugar with lemon juice, serve with vanilla ice-cream and berries • lemon sugar: thinly pare the rind of a lemon and place in the sugar bowl; for a more intense aroma: grate the zest with sugar cubes

garlic

French: ail; Italian: aglio; Spanish: ajo
Garlic is sensual—and taboo for some. But not for Basic cooks, because it adds a lot of flavor to all the healthy culinary pleasures. However: garlic that is too old, has dried, or sprouted really tastes foul. Even worse: garlic powder. OK: garlic on the breath—for both partners
I d e a s : garlic in oil—every drop adds flavor • rub a salad bowl with garlic • push a garlic clove on a fork and beat eggs with it • cook potatoes or rice with garlic and bay leaves • garlic as a side dish: roast whole in foil or fry the cloves or braise them in wine • slice of bread with butter, fresh garlic, and tomatoes

canned tomatoes

Sometimes even star chefs grab a can of tomatoes that is often better for cooking than fresh ones. Whole tomatoes are ideal for prolonged cooking, chopped ones for fast dishes and as a topping; passata doesn't have as much flavor; tomato paste gives concentration
I d e a s : dip made out of butter, tomato paste, Parmesan cheese, garlic, and basil on crackers • braised dishes with peeled tomatoes, very italiano • toast with salami, diced tomato, and mozzarella instead of pizza • fish with peeled tomatoes • canned beans with diced tomatoes to accompany roast chicken

soy sauce

French: sauce soja/soui; Italian: salsa soia; Spanish: salsa soja
Each Asian village has its own brew of soybeans. Soy freaks have all sorts of different soy sauces in their cupboards: the strong dark and salty light ones from China, the sweet and sour one from Indonesia, and the light mild one from Japan. The latter is an absolute Basic.
I d e a s : Asian dip made of soy sauce, ginger, and garlic • cabbage salad with soy sauce • chicken broth with soy sauce • rub fish with soy sauce and fry • marinate meat for grilling in soy sauce • mushrooms in soy sauce • omlette with soy sauce

pesto

Untranslatable
In the old days, only Ligurian mammas used to flavor their dishes with a paste of basil, garlic, pine nuts, olive oil, and Parmesan or Pecorino cheese. Nowadays it's a must-have from New York to Sydney. The more the ingredients of a bought pesto match the ingredients of the original recipe, the better—and more expensive—the pesto is. The Basic recipe is on page 89
I d e a s : potato or pasta salad with pesto • pesto on a tomato and mozzarella sandwich • gnocchi with pesto • tomato and bean soup with pesto • grilled eggplant with pesto • rub chicken with pesto before roasting • cold cuts with pesto • cream cheese with pesto

balsamic vinegar

ood balsamic vinegar is made of fine grape
ice, fermented twice, and left to mature. The
est one, the "tradizionale," is at least 12 years
ld. But good average ones also have the
haracteristic sweet, full flavor and are indeed
alm for the tongue, a salad, and much more.
rice: It's more expensive than other vinegars.
 it isn't, it won't taste any different
Ideas: bruschetta with Parmesan and
 dash of balsamic vinegar • finely sliced
ushrooms with balsamic vinegar • improve
teak and white wine sauces with balsamic
inegar • strawberries with balsamic vinegar
nd basil

curry

Don't worry, take curry. If it is good, meaning
spicy and aromatic, it stimulates (paste more
than powder) and adds oriental magic to many
dishes. The Basics of the world's most famous
spice mix: turmeric (for the yellow color),
cloves, cardamom, cilantro, cumin, paprika,
nutmeg, cinnamon—and chili to varying
degrees, depending on how hot you like it.
Ideas: sprinkle curry on boiled rice, smells
and tastes good • fish soup with curry and
coconut milk • tomato soup with curry • curry
for lamb • curry yogurt marinade for grilled
meat • cook cauliflower, white cabbage,
carrots or zucchini with curry

capers

*French: câpres; Italian: cappei; Spanish:
alcaparrones*
You either love or hate them. If you love the
caper shrub's buds, you know what happiness
means: In brine or salt capers keep their special
flavor forever, ready to give fine food an earthy
touch and turn rustic fare into something really
special. The smaller the caper, the finer it is.
Tiny "nonpareils" are almost like caviar, caper
berries are ideal for tapas
Ideas: vinaigrette with capers • caper
butter with garlic, parsley, lemon rind • sour
cream with pesto and capers • tomato sauce
with capers and tuna • veal goulash in caper
and mustard cream sauce • salmon tartare
with capers

toast

act: Nutritionists don't necessarily recommend
. Here's another fact: Toast can save you from
tarving to death. Slices of toast directly out
f the freezer are so easy—a toaster will bring
em back to life in a matter of seconds, fresh
ir in minutes. And then there's no stopping us.
propose a toast to that!
deas: fry diced toast in butter, making
outons for salads • spaghetti with garlic
outons • quick bake: Mix diced toast with
rips of ham and eggs, bake in the oven
really nice: to coat meat or fish with toast
umbs • dip toast in a sweet egg and milk
ixture and fry for french toast

the quick 17
Basics for the ultimate kick

parsley

*French: persil; Italian: prezzemolo; Spanish:
perejil*
Curly parsley nowadays provokes giggling
at cold buffets; the flat-leaved one, however,
seems to be all the rage: "Pedro's parsley
pesto is divine!" True. And that's why parsley
is our green top model. Also tasty: the white
root. And: Curly parsley can also be very nice
Ideas: parsley salad with cherry tomatoes
• hot apple chutney with parsley • fried sliced
parsley roots with parsley pesto (page 89)
• parsley cream soup, also with the roots
• Asian soups with parsley • parsley gnocchi
• spinach and parsley, half and half, enjoyed
as a side dish

honey

rench: miel; Italian: miele: Spanish: miel
oney stands for natural sweetness with a lot
f flavor—and a lot of different flavors depending
n its origin. Ranging from the resinous flavor
f woodland honey to the basic rather neutral
aste of clover honey. If heated, honey is just
lain sweet. That's why cold-extracted honey
astes better and expensive honey is a waste
f money for cooking
deas: raw vegetables with a ginger honey
ream • red cabbage with a honey vinaigrette
baked goat's cheese with honey • chicken
ings marinated in honey and soy sauce •
acon on toast with honey • honey mustard
ith dill and shrimp

chocolate

*French: chocolat; Italian: ciocolatta; Spanish:
chocolate*
No question—for the Basic kitchen chocolate
means happiness. Even if you don't like it,
bittersweet is ideal for baking and cooking,
because it is purer (contains at least 50 %
cocoa, the more the better). Even better: fat
glazing chocolate. Also good: pure cocoa powder
Ideas: heat cream with chocolate, then whip
• make curls out of glazing chocolate with
peeler • chocolate chips in dough • make
cocoa with your favorite chocolate • dip
strawberries in melted chocolate • cocoa in
pancake batter • cook pasta in sweetened
vanilla milk and add some chocolate

mustard

*French: moutarde; Italian: mostarda; Spanish:
mostaza*
Just like honey and soy sauce, mustard comes
in many variations, but still tastes like mustard.
Basic is a rather mild mustard; purer, however,
is a strong mustard. Sweet mustard is for
connoisseurs, coarse mustard goes especially
well with cold cuts
Ideas: lettuce with apples and mustard
cream • dip made of strong mustard, mixed
pickles, and crème fraîche to go with cold meat
• smoked salmon rolls with mustard • slice
a frankfurter, mix with coarse mustard and
chives, eat in French bread • spread mustard
on meat or fresh fish, coat in flour, and fry

Preparing
a meal

"I'll cook something!"
But how...?

Take potatoes for example. They can be cooked, peeled or in their skins, in water, or in stock. They can also be roasted, sliced, diced, whole, raw or cooked. And they can be baked. And braised. And grilled, broiled, steamed, fried, "au gratin," deep-fried. Help! That sounds like work, like a lot of work.

Be Basic. You can't do everything at once, and anyway, you only want to achieve one thing: heat up something raw to turn it into something edible and tasty. Water, electricity, and gas play the leading roles in this. Water can smooth and penetrate or drench and wear out. Energy provides speed—but too much energy can end up in a smoking disaster. Use a lot of water and little energy for a delicate bite (gentle simmering). Use no water and a lot of energy for a crispy crust (deep-frying). Between these two poles lies the whole wide world of cooking. Welcome!

Rapid boiling

That means: masses of energy and water, because the ingredients need a lot of heat and liquid over a very short period of time to be cooked properly. Like pasta for example. Or broccoli.

A saucepan needs three things

Do you want to boil a jumbo-sized pack of pasta or just an egg? Only very rarely will you cook more than that or less than that. Two saucepans are all you need—for that and for everything in between: a small one that holds 1 quart of water (and fits nicely on the small burner), and a big one which can hold 4–5 quarts (for the big burner). But if you cook quite often and are not too enthusiastic about dishwashing, you should add another two saucepans: a small high one for 2 quarts of soup and a wide big one for 3 quarts and lots of potatoes.

You do not need expensive special equipment for boiling. But your Basic saucepan shouldn't be made of tin either. You can't go wrong with stainless steel, but an enamel pot will also last you a long time. A heavy bottom is good and, being quite resistant, it will not produce spots in the pan after long hours of cooking. The pan must fit properly on the burner for the heat to spread evenly. Good handles won't drop off or mind oven temperatures. And a good lid will keep the heat in the pan.

What else do you need for cooking? A wooden spoon for stirring, a skimming ladle for removing, and a colander for draining. And salt.

A generous portion of salt

Rapid boiling usually takes place in salted water. Good stock would be a waste—it simply couldn't give off its rich aroma in such a short time. A lot of salt is also used in blanching (will be explained later), so that the food can get a fair share of it. Last but not least, we'll let you in on a secret: Bring water to a boil, add the raw ingredients, and only then add salt—this way it will go back to a boil sooner.

Into the boiling water

A chef may from time to time fry something as basic as a pork chop, and a cookbook may also contain recipes for raw foods. But here we're talking about the real stuff: cooking at 212 °F in hot and bubbling water. The aim: well-cooked food with a bite but no crust. How: pretty wet, pretty hot, pretty short. What happens: The starch in pasta swells up to a real bite, the cellulose structure in vegetables breaks down. In both cases the heat releases the flavor and the salted water spreads it evenly. But if cooked too long, firm stuff will become mushy and tasty stuff will become inedible. One exception: the egg—it turns from liquid to firm and will stay that way, even after an hour's cooking.

Rapid boiling has one big disadvantage: nutrients and flavor can drown in boiling water.

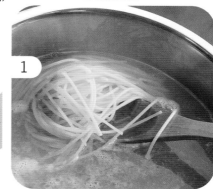
1

Steaming may be an option, but delicate foods may lose even more flavor. It's best to get the rapid boiling over with as quickly as possible: Use a lot of water, so it won't stop bubbling when the food is thrown in (important for delicate sugar snaps for example). And make sure the pieces are similar in size and texture.

Cooking pasta

For each 1/4 pound of pasta bring 1 quart of water to a boil, using a big saucepan. Add the pasta and the salt (1 heaped teaspoon per quart) and stir vigorously. The pasta tends to stick in the beginning. The water must be brought back to a boil quickly, and then continue to gently bubble. Do not cover the saucepan, and and keep on stirring occasionally (1).

The cooking time depends on the type of pasta and the brand (follow the instructions on the package). On average it takes about 8–13 minutes. Toward the end you need to try the pasta by fishing out a few bits (2). If it's still too firm to the bite, continue cooking, if it is *al dente*, pour it straight into the colander!

Italians would now place the pasta in a hot bowl, add the sauce, and serve immediately—no need for a cold shower in between. But if you insist, quickly (!) rinse the pasta under hot (!!) water. As a general rule, remember: Guests and sauce can wait, but pasta doesn't like to be kept waiting. And it doesn't like cold plates either. Here's a little trick: Just before the end of cooking, pour one ladle of cooking water onto the plates. But don't forget to pour it out afterward!

Cooking potatoes

If you cook potatoes in their skins, thoroughly wash and brush them under running water. Place them in a saucepan and cover with cold water, add salt. Cover and bring to a boil, reduce the heat, and cook gently for 20–30 minutes, depending on the size. Rinse the

2

potatoes under cold water and leave them to cool down a little. Peel the potatoes while they are still hot.

If you want to cook peeled potatoes, you obviously have to peel and wash them beforehand. Cut into pieces of roughly the same size—and cook them immediately. Place them in a saucepan, cover with cold salted water, bring to a boil, cover, and gently cook for 15–20 minutes, depending on size. Drain and and leave to stand briefly uncovered (do not rinse them!).

Cooking vegetables

Place the vegetable, cut into pieces of roughly the same size (e.g. beans, broccoli florets, asparagus), in plenty of salted water and cook until tender but still firm to the bite. Robust vegetables can drain in a colander, delicate ones should be removed from the water using a slotted spoon or skimming ladle.

Blanching is very quick: Immerse the vegetable briefly first in boiling water and then in ice water with ice cubes (3). The cold shock brings out the color and helps to keep the texture. It does, however, take away some of the flavor. Nevertheless, it's a must for casseroles, gratins, or quiches. And before freezing.

3

Gentle simmering

Gentle simmering brings extremes together since it is the finest and largest pieces of an animal which are best cooked just below 212 °F: filet and leg meat; chicken breast and boiling chicken. Fish. (And dumplings.)

Pots and pans for big and small

You don't need different pots or pans for gentle simmering rather than rapid boiling. However they should be the right size! This means that pieces of food should not touch the hot edges, but shouldn't get lost in the sauce either. To poach (explanation later) a chicken breast, a saucepan with a handle, as you would use for cooking milk, should do the job. A coddled (we'll also explain this later on) beefsteak or dumplings for friends and family will need more space, upward of 5 quarts.

Because gently cooked foods need to be handled gently, remember that fish in particular cooks best barely covered and in a shallow saucepan where it can be accessed easily. If you are planning for a big festivity and need to cook a whole fish, it's best to use an oval-shaped vessel—also useful for steaming, or for cooking asparagus.

Forks are absolutely forbidden in gentle cooking. Instead, use a skimming ladle for big pieces and a slotted spoon to preserve everything else. A ladle and a fine strainer are absolutely necessary if you want to use the delicious stock.

Good stock

Gentle cooks mostly cook only with water—at least when cooking something big like a boiled chicken. Spices, herbs, and soup vegetables are only added later. For short cooking, it's best to cook the stock in advance. A good brew for fish, for example, can be made of water, wine, onions, soup vegetables, bay leaves, a few peppercorns as well as a good old lemon—both juice and zest.

Poaching and coddling

Auguste Escoffier, the world's first celebrity chef, called gentle cooking "cooking without cooking." It nearly drove him to distraction that he was unable to find a better definition. It lies somewhere between simmering and soft boiling. Make sure the temperature in the pan doesn't reach 212 °F, since it would then become normal boiling. This method of preparation is called "poaching" for small and tender, quickly cooked pieces and "coddling" for larger pieces. First aid: Keep a cup of cold water within reach of the stove—should the water boil over, quickly use it to reduce the temperature.

Lowest coddling temperature lies at around 175 °F, because, below that, your food will spoil more than cook. However, never let the temperature rise above 200 °F and approach boiling point. If a piece of meat, for example, which was meant for slow cooking, is

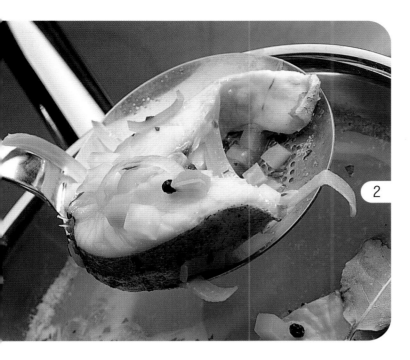

2

boiled, its cell structure will begin to collapse, its fibers will start to fall apart, and in the end all that will be left to eat will be tasteless chewy stringy fibers. However, if it is cooked just below 200 °F, it will be juicy, firm, and tender.

It's even worse with fish, since that immediately falls to pieces in boiling water and becomes as dry as straw. It is therefore very important to reach the correct temperature and stay there.

Coddling stewing meat

Use at least 2 good pounds of beef for the lengthy cooking time to be worthwhile and to produce good stock. To give your meat and stock even more taste, cook beef bones for an hour beforehand. Which meat to use: Most suitable for this are pieces from flank, ribs, shoulder, and leg.

Now it's really quite easy: Gently bring water (1 quart for each pound of meat) with an onion or some garlic to a boil and add the meat. Adjust the stove's temperature so that the brew won't bubble, but some movement on its surface should be visible. Ideally, this should happen after about 20 minutes and then last for about

2–3 hours, as long as your stove keeps an even temperature. The meat will be soft on the outside, tender and juicy inside. Season with salt when served. If you would like some greens with it, then add some soup vegetables an hour before the end of cooking. If you want really aromatic stock, then do this another hour earlier and also add bay leaves, cloves, and a few peppercorns.

It's more or less the same procedure for poultry, except for two things: When you add the poultry, the water must not be boiling (skin tears and outer meat dries up), and the overall cooking time is about $1-1^1/_2$ hours, depending on size.

Poaching fish

The more flesh that is covered by the skin and therefore protected from leaching, the better the poached fish will taste. That's why whole fish or the classic thick haddock pieces are particularly suitable for this type of cooking. But a filet can also be delicious in a strong brew (see left on how to make this).

Bring stock to a boil and remove from heat. As soon as it stops bubbling, add the fish—not too much though: Never stack the pieces and add just enough so that the stock won't cool down too much (1). Put the pan back on the heat and poach the fish. There will be some movement in the stock, but it should all be beneath the surface. Depending on thickness, the fish will be ready after 2–5 minutes (2). Tender meat such as chicken breasts or filets can also be cooked this way—although cooking time is of course a little longer.

1

Big whole fish like carp are placed in cold stock and then put on the heat to allow the temperature to disperse evenly; smaller fish like trout are added to hot stock. From then on it takes about 5–8 minutes, but sometimes up to 10–20 minutes for big ones.

Stewing & steaming

Excellent for tender stuff: cooking with little or no liquid, for the full taste to land on your plate and not in the sink. Great for vegetables and fish.

Cooking on two levels

For stewing, the lid is more important than the pot. It must fit tightly enough to allow almost nothing to escape the pot and to let all the flavors meet, communicate, and intermingle in this tropical climate. The pot itself? Just an ordinary saucepan, large enough to spread out all the ingredients so that they'll cook evenly.

You can also use a pot like this for steaming, but you will also need a coffee cup and a saucer (more about that on the next page). Expert steamers, however, prefer the stacked steaming pot: The bottom pot is flat, onto which another perforated pot fits perfectly. A good lid sits tightly on the perforated pot. Water boils on the bottom level and it steam-cooks whatever is on the top level! It's better to use steam inserts like the Asian bamboo steaming baskets, which you can put in a wok or a wide saucepan. Even a pasta colander can do the trick—but only without its handle to allow the lid to close properly.

A little liquid

Stewing is about give and take: The liquid gives the ingredients heat and sometimes flavor, the ingredients give the liquid nutrients and flavor in return. As a thank you, both are served! The more intense the liquid, the greater the pleasure. It can be mineral water (real snobs have their specific brand), stock, wine, cream, or sauce. Ordinary tap water is usually used for steaming, but intense herbs and spices are also used here for flavoring.

Stewing & steaming

It's not quite clear what stewing is all about. Is it boiling, or more steaming, maybe even braising? Amazingly enough, less water is needed for longer and gentler cooking. Some vitamins and flavors don't handle this very well, but you do get stock as an extra. While stewing vegetables or fish, they give so much flavor that you obtain a really strong broth. If you also use fat, it will taste heavenly.

Steaming is a lot clearer. Water boils, but the ingredients only come into contact with the steam. Advantage: pure taste, hardly anything is lost in cooking water. But this can be seen as a disadvantage by flavor freaks. Some also doubt that steam is gentler on the ingredients, since steam burns

2

3

more severely than boiling water. This is true as is the fact that steaming takes longer than boiling. Nevertheless: what's lost in heat and cooking time is less than what gets lost in the stock during cooking.

Stewing vegetables

Nearly all vegetables can be stewed, other than particularly hard ones such as legumes. All pieces must be of the same size. If everything goes according to plan, at the end of cooking the stock will have reduced to a concentrated essence and will stick to the cooked vegetables.

More or less liquid is used, depending on cooking time: Carrots are just covered (1), spinach is thrown into the pot with only the few drops of the water it was rinsed in clinging to its leaves. You definitely need a lid for slow simmering at a low heat. You also need to stir if the pot is quite full, so that each piece can get its fair share of steam and stock.

Glazed vegetables are a delicacy. Stew them with butter and sugar, remove the lid a few minutes before the end of cooking, and reduce quickly until everything is covered—glazed—with shiny syrup. If you want, you can add a bit of fresh butter at the end. Great for slightly sweet vegetables like white cabbage and carrots. Also de luxe: stewing with cream. This often tastes best with simple vegetables like leek or kohlrabi.

Stewing fish

Cook a good 1 cup of fish stock for gentle cooking (pages 22/23), 1/2 cup white wine, and a few onion rings, just enough to cover the bottom by about the width of a finger, for about two minutes over a high heat. Remove onions and add salted filets or small whole fish placed side by side.

Now cook everything over a low heat, cover with a lid or—hint!— cover the fish directly with buttered foil. Or use the butter wrapper. Depending on size, filets are done after 2–6 minutes, whole fish after a maximum of 10 minutes. Add some cream to the stock, and there's your sauce! If you would rather the XL-version (extremely luscious), stew the vegetables with the fish.

1

Steaming vegetables

The cooking water must not come too close to the vegetables. This gives water the chance to boil really fast and produce lots of steam under the lid. Big compact heaps of vegetables are a no-no, since the steam won't reach everywhere. Steaming takes about one third to one half the time again as standard cooking. Season only at the end.

Steaming fish

It's best to use Asian bamboo steaming baskets. Line them with salad or cabbage leaves, add herbs and spices, then the seasoned fish—preferably whole, in which case it needs be cut open on the sides (2). Filets can also be steamed.

Let water evaporate into steam in a wok or a large saucepan and put closed steaming baskets inside. A fish of around 1 1/2 pounds is done after about 15–20 minutes, filets take 5–6 minutes. Anything else? Oh yes, the magic trick with cup and saucer for occasional steamers (3): In a pot with a little boiling water, place the coffee cup upside down, and lay the saucer with the fish on top of the cup, put the lid on, and steam. Very Basic!

Quick frying

For a piece of meat or fish to be quickly crispy, you need to panfry it. This cooking technique is also good for vegetables, pasta, eggs — and of course for fried potatoes.

Two skillets and a spatula

You need two skillets in the Basic kitchen: one for light, delicate things and one for the bigger stuff. Lighter things such as fish, vegetables, or egg dishes are best fried in nonstick pans. Many types and brands are available, but the end result is always the same: What goes in must come out, and nothing must stick to the pan. That's it.

You therefore have to look after your pan. Avoid stirring with metal utensils and cleaning it with a wire pad, because you'll scratch away the pan's coating. Also avoid excessive cooking temperatures. The nonstick protection will disappear above medium temperatures or above 425 °F in the oven. And the traditional three-year-warranty doesn't cover this. What else do you need to know? Yes, a heavy bottom is more heat resistant and won't deform as easily.

To sear a steak, you need pure metal, i.e. an uncoated frying pan. Experts use cast-iron pans; at home stainless-steel pans with heavy bottoms are more common. New alloys are available these days. Uncoated pans are very sensitive after frying: They don't appreciate dish liquid, since this will destroy the built-up grease layer. Wiping out (and if necessary, rinsing with water) and greasing keeps them at their best. When a metal pan really "runs," it becomes a collectors' piece. And attains a collectors' price!

If after all that you still turn your steak with a fork, you will lose what's most important: the juice will just ooze out of the meat. It is better to turn it with a spatula or with a normal tablespoon.

A generous portion of fat

Use margarine or butter for shallow-frying, for scrambled eggs, or fish, for example. Clarified butter or ghee can take a little more heat. If you want to get really hot, you need to use high-temperature vegetable shortening. You can still add a piece of butter or a splash of olive oil at the end for more flavor.

Onto the heat

What happens during quick frying? When the food is thrown into the pan, it is exposed to high levels of heat immediately. Protein coagulates instantly, and a protective skin forms on the outside that can later turn into a crust. Inside, it cooks slowly and evenly. The result: Your steak is full of flavor and a pink center on your plate.

Two things mean trouble when frying: smoke and water. Smoke develops when the pan gets too hot. This is easily dealt with. If, on the the other hand, the pan is too cold, the protective skin forms too late for the liquid to stay inside. Meat and fish will stew instead of frying, and that will make them dry out. Not the sort of thing we want on our plates, thank you!

1

It sounds terrible. But luckily it is avoidable if you know what to do. First heat the pan. Only then add the fat. It will heat up faster, without burning. When you add the pieces of food, they must sizzle gently. If this is the case, you have hit the right temperature. It's best to try this with a small piece first. If the pan is too hot, it can easily burn. And if too cool, the result will be too much liquid, dried-out food.

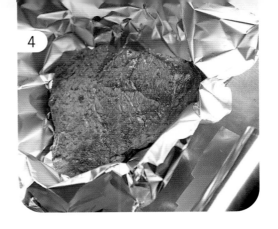

Panfrying fish filets

Wash fish under cold running cold water, pat dry, and salt before frying. You can add lemon, but it's not essential. If you flour your filets lightly, it will give them a light crust and some firmness.

Heat fat in a nonstick pan at a medium temperature and add the filets with their best side down, so that they will be facing up after turning. Fry for about 1 minute, until browned underneath, and turn. Fry for another minute and baste with frying fat.

As soon as the filet feels firm to the finger (just poke it gently), remove it. Even if you think it could use a little longer in the pan, still take it out! Fish always fries faster than you think. Only thick pieces, like salmon for example, need a bit longer.

Panfrying steaks

To panfry a steak, it must be at least 2/3 inch thick, 1–1 1/2 inches for a filet steak. Salt and pepper the steak after frying, although there's nothing wrong with doing it beforehand.

Heat up fat in an uncoated pan, without letting it smoke. Add the steaks—they should really sizzle. Fry for about 1 minute, turn, fry for another minute, and then leave to rest for a few minutes next to the cooker. Now cook the steaks at a medium temperature and turn often (1–3). For thick steaks, you can also put them in a 430 °F hot oven—there they'll cook nicely and evenly. After 6–8 minutes in a pan, a 5 ounce pork steak is done and a 7 ounce beefsteak is pink.

The steak will be even more tender if you let it rest for a few minutes either in foil between preheated plates (4) or in a 120 °F hot oven.

Roasting
& braising

This is mostly for meat, lots of meat, lots of tender meat. It only really becomes tasty after a long time in the oven or stewpot.

Heavy metal for good cooking

If you take the time to roast or braise, then you'll probably want to go the whole way! Invite some friends, put the pork roast in the oven, and go back to bed. Exceptionally, you'll need a little more than a basic pot for this. But there's no need to invest in a Rolls-Royce model at half the price of a stove.

The right pot for this sort of event is an oval casserole with a lid and a thick base, in which your roast has plenty of space and can braise for quite some time. They're available for the price of a fresh Christmas turkey. A Dutch oven, which won't burn easily, will do for braising stews. If it is ovenproof (metal handles!), then everything is possible! And: Keep ladle and strainer at hand for basting.

Use good ingredients, get good sauce

For most people, the best thing about braising is the sauce, which gets its flavor from all that's in the pot besides meat. You will most often find onions, which provide color and an earthy taste. Other classics are diced root vegetables. Tomatoes give a Mediterranean touch. And now on o the liquid. Wine and stock give power. Add a little water and it makes them a little less

potent. Add whole spices at the start and herbs at the end of the cooking time—the more delicate the herbs are, the later they are added in order to preserve their fragrant aromas.

Slowly does it

The same rule applies to frying as to cooking: the hotter, the faster. With meat, the rule only applies to tender pieces. Their structure is so delicate that they can just about bear strong heat before being done— rare to pink on the inside, nice and crusty on the outside. Less tender roasting meat will look similar, but because of its rough fibers, it will not have the same texture. But if it is cooked more gently and for longer after searing, it will become juicy.

This is what happens when roasting a roast: When searing, juice flows out first of all, then that dries up to form a crust. As the remaining juice is trapped because the meat is now sealed, it flows to the core and, on its way there, cooks the meat. The closer the juice gets to the core, the less rare the roast.

When braising, liquid—added after searing—covers the whole roast, bubbling and steaming, which in turn gives a lot of its flavor to the braising liquid. You obtain a tender work of art and a delicious sauce. If many pieces are braised instead of just the one, it's generally called a stew, or goulash, or ragout. But the principle is the same, whatever you call it.

Roasting a roast

Season the roast and sear it in hot fat (1)—on top of the stove (quicker) or directly in a 480 °F oven (more evenly). Quick searing is enough for tender pieces, but other cuts may need some more time, up to a maximum of half an hour.

It gets a little cooler after searing: 350 °F is good for the "hot & fast" method, "soft & slow" is between 300 °F and 175 °F. This is called "low-heat" cooking and allows the meat to cook evenly for a long time. Minutes don't really count for much here. Fatty roasts, like a Christmas turkey, shouldn't be roasted too gently, because the fat will turn soft rather than crispy.

Two things are important for roasting a roast: During roasting, baste regularly to prevent the crust from burning. Afterward, leave it to rest to allow the juices, which flowed to the center, to disperse throughout the roast and the heated fibers to relax.

Braising a roast

Braising is always "soft and slow" and is ideal for lean, rough-fibered pieces. Sear as above, but not in such a big pan, so that less liquid will be necessary later on. Brown vegetables, and then, depending on cooking time, add corresponding liquids and spices. Don't cover the roast completely or it will simply boil (2). Put the lid on and let everything braise in sauce and steam, as for coddling. Experts do this in the oven, because the heat is more regular. It can also be done on top of the stove, but the roast must then be turned regularly.

When the roast is ready, cover it with foil and place it to rest in the turned-off oven, while you are making the sauce: Spoon out all the fat (3), strain through a fine strainer, and season to taste.

Braising a stew

Similar to braising a roast: First sear the meat, one piece after another for large quantities, because otherwise it will cook too fast. Remove the meat. Sauté the vegetables—usually onions—until they are transparent, put the meat back in, and season. It's the other way around for goulash.

Now for the important bit: Dishes that require long braising, like beef ragout, only need their own juice in the beginning and a few dashes of water during cooking to become really tender. Add the rest of the liquid at the end. Things that take less time —chicken pieces for example—are braised with all their liquids from the start.

Wok & deep-frying

Time for some heat. Because there's no action in woks or deep-frying pans under 212 °F, quick hands and alert responses are required. The rewards are meat, fish, and vegetables that are crispy on the outside, tender on the inside, and have lots of flavor all over.

Hot stuff

Which wok to choose? It depends: Thin-walled ones are ideal for stirring quickly and withstanding strong heat. In Asia, they're made of sheet iron and have a round bottom, which transfers heat very well over a fire. This type of wok can be used on our stoves too with a special ring, although our gas cookers aren't as hot as a Chinese fire. A better alternative is the version for electric ranges, with a flat bottom. The ideal diameter is 14 inches. Sheet-steel woks are cheap and do their job pretty well. Wash them with water and grease them to keep them going. Unfortunately, they can dent. Thin stainless-steel woks are better (but more expensive). Or just get another new cheap sheet-steel wok. Heavy cast-iron woks react more slowly and are ideal for braising. And if you really want to get cooking with a wok, then you also need the special round-edged wok scoop and the wok ladle. All this can be found in Asian stores which sell good woks. You don't need a lid for stir-frying, but you do need one for braising, steaming, and cooking. A wok can do all that. And fry.

And even deep-fry. (Did you know that?) Deep-fry in a wok? Asian fries? Why not. You don't necessarily need a deep-fryer for deep-frying in fat. You can even do it with less fat in a wok. A large saucepan could also do the job, provided it's high enough to be half-filled with fat. Large things can be easily fished out with a suitable wire basket or strainer. For more delicate stuff, use a slotted spoon or skimming ladle.

Either a lot of spices or a lot of fat

The real wok cook needs three things: ginger, garlic, and scallions—the basic ingredients for many—most?—Asian stir-fried dishes. Sauces and pastes, such as soy, fish, or oyster sauces, curry or shrimp pastes, spice everything up at the end of cooking. None of this must be added while deep-frying, because they would immediately burn and ruin the fat. The fat itself needs to be quite resistant, and must be able to withstand high temperatures and have little taste of its own. Plain vegetable oil is perfect.

Hot & tasty

In stir-frying, the hottest area of the wok is the bottom bulge. Vegetables and meat get a crust there instantly and the juices immediately bubble underneath. Small pieces are cooked in no time. Because minutes and millimeters count here, everything must be chopped—preferably very finely—well in advance of cooking and laid out ready for stir-frying. Assemble the ingredients in separate heaps or small bowls and you can't go wrong. Remember to constantly stir the vegetables, since otherwise they will burn. (This is of course why it's known as stir-frying!) Swirling and whirling is what is required here. Expert wok cooks use the cooler wok walls to keep cooked items warm.

Deep-frying is just another term for cooking in fat. And as it only gets going from 350 °F onward, the crust forms quickly, underneath which juices rise—the same as in wok cooking.

For the food to be tasty, these two rules must be followed to the letter. Number one: The bigger the piece, the more slowly it must be cooked; otherwise the crust will burn and the inside will remain cold. Number two: the right temperature. If the fat is too cold, crusts form late (= too late) and everything soaks itself full of fat. If it's too hot and smokes, then everything is crispy before being done and black when done. Easy test: Put a piece of bread into the fat. If it's golden-brown wand crispy after about one minute, then you have the right temperature (1).

Wok-cooking vegetables

Wok-cooking, or stir-frying, is only really possible in Asian pans. Rule: The firmer the texture, the thinner the cut. Therefore only roughly chop spinach, but finely chop carrots. Prepare everything beforehand, even the salt and soy sauce. When wok-cooking, there's no time for anything else, like stopping and searching.

Beginner's wok-cooking: Heat the wok up hot. You have the right temperature when a drop of water can perform a tap dance. If it disappears without a great show, then the wok needs some more heat. Now rinse the hot wok with oil, then add and heat a little oil. Add vegetables, the ones which need to cook longest first. Remember to keep tossing and stirring to avoid burning. Add the next set of vegetables—the ones with a shorter cooking time—keep tossing and stirring, add other vegetables, and so on. If every vegetable has the same degree of firmness at the end, you've done it right! If not, it still tastes great and you'll do better next time around. You can now add spices and sauces and then serve immediately.

Advanced wok-cooking: Start as above, then sear vegetable number one and push up on the wok walls, add vegetable number two, sear, mix with vegetable number one, everything goes up the walls again. Add vegetable number three, and so on. Important in both versions: Nothing must lie on top of each other! About 1 pound of ingredients can be wok-cooked at once.

Deep-frying vegetable tempura

Things that contain a lot of starch like potatoes or pasta can be deep-fried without problems. Things that are more delicate or contain more water need a little extra help from dough or batter. The Japanese tempura batter is ideal for this.

Before making the batter, you need to cut the vegetables into bite-size pieces and quickly cook the firm ones over high heat. Heat about 1 quart of fat to 350 °F (to find out how see left). In the meantime, make the batter: Carefully mix 1 2/3 cups ice-cold water (ideally put the water in the freezer until just before freezing point) with 2 egg yolks and then with 2 cups flour. Don't worry about lumps; long and heavy stirring is fatal!

Now coat the vegetables with flour and dip them in the batter (2). Let it drip off and immediately afterward put it in the hot fat. Only cover the surface to avoid the fat cooling down. Everything is cooked and crispy after only 1–2 minutes. Remove with a skimming ladle (3), place on paper towels to absorb excess fat and then season with salt. Keep warm in the oven at 165 °F. Reheat fat and continue.

knife

pepper mill

chopping boar

the
fantastic
14

Basics
for the
ultimate twist

grater

whisk

kettle

peeler

measuring cup

blender

can opener

cork screw

colander

lemon squeezer

radio

knife

We need to be strict here: If you think you're ruling the roost with a $10.00 knife block, then you're totally mistaken. It's simply too cheap to be good. It is so much better to have just three knives, but three knives of high quality which will last you a lifetime: a small one for small stuff, such as peeling onions, a bigger one with a longer, thinner blade for everything from cutting a steak to trimming broccoli, and one with a really big and wide blade. With this one, you can hold its handle and your hand won't touch the chopping board. This is ideal for slicing and chopping fresh herbs. This knife alone will, however, cost you more than a whole block. But it will definitely last longer than all the knives in the famous knife block!

pepper mill

Freshly ground pepper or ground pepper from a bag? If you couldn't care less about this, you probably adore the passion of dime novels. Coming fresh from the mill, peppercorns are more than just spicy—and they are definitely not musty. And since it's really Basic to get a great effect with just one twist, a proper pepper mill is an absolute must in the Basic kitchen. Proper doesn't necessarily mean a stunning design. Proper means an efficient grinding mechanism! Please choose the classic outdated wood model with adjustable grinding levels and not the classy plastic pyramid, which always slips out of your wet hands and is as difficult to open and refill as a pharaoh's grave.

chopping board

To cut tomatoes directly on the kitchen table oozes real country living, but is simply a mess. The Basic kitchen needs a chopping board. And if possible a second one for strong stuff like garlic. You wouldn't want your fruit salad to taste of garlic, would you? If you can cut an iceberg lettuce on your Basic board without loads of it falling off, it will be big enough for most things. If it's made out of plastic, it's very practical. You can put it in the dishwasher. If it's made of wood, it looks nice, but will need special attention. If you love scrubbing choose a wooden one. Avoid: a board with a groove (impossible to clean), a bizarrely shaped board (everything falls off), a board with feet (use a damp cloth instead).

the fantastic 14

Basics for the ultimate twist

grater

We'll only mention one thing: Parmesan. Freshly grated, Parmesan turns nearly everything into something special. This is why a grater is an absolute must in the Basic kitchen. Best is the Basic, ordinary model— a four-sided semi-box. You can grate cheese with it or nutmeg for soup, an apple for sauce or lemon zest for cake. You can even use it as a skimming ladle or a wok ladle. It will also grate carrots, or finely slice cucumber. And with a tea light in the middle, you can even turn it into a lantern...

whisk

There are some really classy accessories for rounding off sauces or whisking gourmet cream creations. But one of these magic objects is quite enough. It must, however, have two things: first, flexible wires, so that beating and whisking won't kill you, and you can whisk air into the mixture; second, a handle with a proper grip, that won't fall off after long use or have a secret compartment for retaining dishwater. And now to the secret of hand-frothed cappuccino: In a small high pot bring full-fat milk (skimmed milk is for stingy people only) to a boil, take the whisk and whisk, whisk, whisk. The foam will be so solid that any sugar you add will stay on top.

kettle

Even if these are not used very often in the U.S.A, we thought we'd include this very British kitchen accessory—it's just so useful! Once you've discovered the mixture of immersion heater and water pot, you'll never want to give up. If you're not an early riser, you'll really appreciate it—while you're still half asleep, it'll boil your tea water in seconds. It also helps chaotic cooks to bring a pan of pasta to the boil in no time. Just take these two warnings seriously: Be cautious with the steam. A scalded hand is even more painful than a burnt one. And always put enough water in the kettle, or it may go funny on you.

peeler

ven if your mother manages to scrape arrots and peel potatoes in no time with little knife, there is a lot to be said for a eeler with a swiveling blade—it will definitely nake life a lot easier. You can even peel things ke peppers or asparagus with it. Vertical r horizontal blade, the choice is yours. 's simply a matter of technique and skill. ou can use all your imagination: For example, eel carrots lengthwise like ribbons or carve pattern in cucumbers—looks really pretty hen cut diagonally. Or, or, or...

measuring cup

If you regard measuring as a bureaucratic nonsense, you're either an expert or too chilled to be cool! This can ruin your cakes. But it can be avoided with a measuring cup, preferably a see-through one. The finer the scale, the better. It should go down to 1/4 cup and even to 1 ounce. For smaller quantities, you can use spoons. Make sure you get a set on a ring, then you'll always have the particular spoon you need to hand.

blender

Was there life before the hand-held blender? It must have been filled with tiresome kneading, grinding, pounding, and vigorous stirring. Now we simply take the blender, press the button and, as if by magic, the shake is mixed, the soup puréed, the sauce smooth. Provided the blender has enough power (which is not always the case with kitchen-aid accessories). And don't forget: Some things also taste good not beaten into a pulp. And some things really don't like to be blended: mashed potato turns tough and slimy, herbs bitter, and whipping cream may turn stiff but certainly not light and airy.

can opener

Why, you may ask ... because the Basic kitchen cannot operate without canned tomatoes is the answer! That's why you need a can opener. If you don't have a Great Dane as a pet, there's no need for an electric one. A can opener just needs to do its job well: to open a can without putting too much strain on the hand or on the brain. An opener with one handle only is a tool for adventurous explorers. It's definitely easier to use a model with two handles: Squeeze the handles together so that the lip around the top of the can is between them and the blade can slice the lid off neatly. It takes a lot of practice, of course. And don't forget: can openers *can* be cleaned...

corkscrew

A bottle opener is the sophisticated brother of a can opener. They have one important thing in common: the easier it is to use, the better. The simple spiral with a handle attached on top is indeed very Basic, but only Mister Muscle finds it easy to use. And as there are not that many of those around, there are some alternatives on offer, luckily. They are much more efficient if the instrument driven into the cork is a real metal helix rather than a big screw. You pull out the cork by either levering it (these corkscrews usually have two arms) or screwing it in the other direction. Some corkscrews do this automatically—then nothing can go wrong. Or find Mister Muscle...

colander

he most important aspect of a colander (or a trainer if you prefer) is its holes. There is the trainer with large holes for quick straining r pressing soft things through, like cooked otatoes. Then there is the fine-meshed ersion, ideal for soups and sauces. (Real nobs strain their stock through paper coffee lters.) Or there is the colander for salad and asta with many big holes. Metal ones are eally good, but not absolutely necessary. 2.99 plastic colanders often render good and aithful service for many years. Another must r all salad fans: the salad spinner.

lemon squeezer

Each household has at least two of these— at the end of each person's arms. But if you want to get to the last drop, squeezing with bare hands is not enough. Ordinary and designer lemon squeezers have one thing in common: a stylish dome, which looks a bit like the tip of a toy rocket. It squeezes the juice out of the fruit and lets it trickle down. If there is nothing to separate the pits and pulp from the juice, it is not a good squeezer. The juice should be strained while being collected. For small quantities, a receptacle at the bottom of the dome will do. A lemon squeezer must be a solid instrument—a lot of force is used when squeezing.

radio

A kitchen without a radio is like a summer without sun: no fun at all. Morning coffee simply tastes better when listening to stupid jokes, and lunch must be accompanied by your favorite songs. You need some opera to make your spaghetti taste really Italian. There's always something on which is of interest, and that is really Basic. The radio itself should be Basic too, i.e. not have lots of switches; otherwise you'll end up spending more time at the radio than at the oven. Very important: a big on–off switch, which can be operated with a wooden spoon, if necessary. But do be careful not to get carried away by the program—dancing skillets and smoldering steaks can get dangerous.

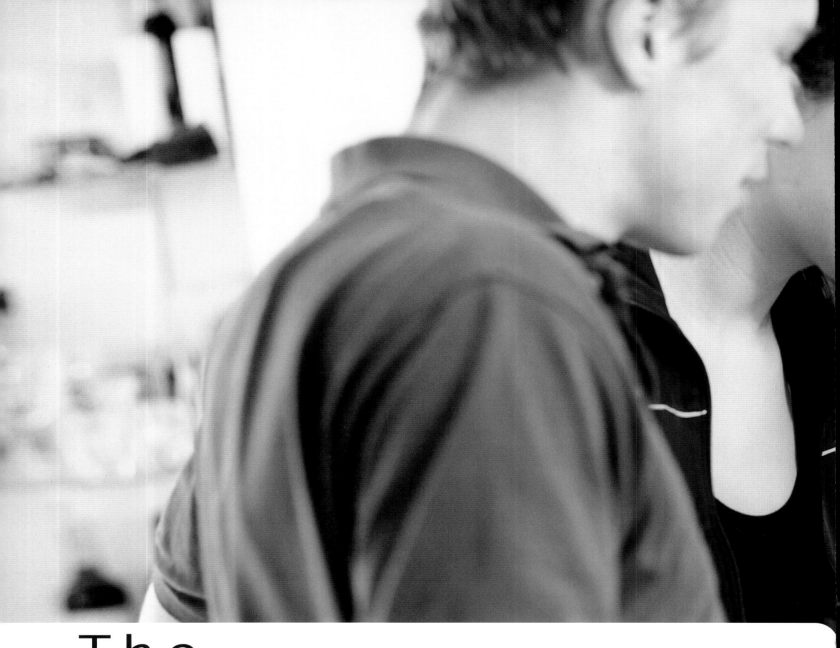

The Recipes

pasta

Pasta
potatoes,

...Something filling. Easy to prepare. Something everybody loves

, & more

Hungry? Fair enough. Over the last 40 pages we had nice long discussions, but now our stomachs are rumbling. No more chitter-chatter please—we would like something to eat. Something nice and filling. Something easy to prepare. Something everybody loves.

What do Italians do in such a situation ? They cook pasta, of course. What else would they do? Cook rice, mainly risotto. In Asia people cook loads of rice—and loads of noodles. But that is exactly the difference. They are called "noodles" and not "pasta."In the U.S.A. people love both, but love fried potatoes even more. However, "French fries" originated in France, or rather in Belgium. Not surprisingly, however, the Irish are the champion potato-eaters. But when it comes to bread, nobody beats the Germans; nowhere else is there more variety. At present their favorites are: Bruschetta, Crostini, Tramezzini. Sounds quite Italian, doesn't it? Mamma mia, we really are hungry.

No more talking. Food please! OK?

Let's start.

Please turn the page.

Bread for the world

A good sandwich can save the day, they say—but what makes a good sandwich? That really depends on the country you are in. In Italy the answer may be *tramezzini*, in France a toasted *croque-monsieur* or (with a fried egg on top) a *croque-madame*, in Sweden an open *smörgåsbord* (possibly on pumpernickel), in Germany a *Wurstbrot* or *Schinkenbrot*! Not to forget the famous American club sandwich—doubledeckers filled to the brim with loads and loads of whatever takes your fancy. Yes, a good sandwich can save the day—but people's culinary dreams can be very different.

Bread for Melissa
A round flatbread sandwich: spread with a paste of chopped green olives and olive oil; add romaine lettuce, slices of fried eggplant, pickled peppers, feta cheese

Bread for Nadya
A pumpernickel sandwich: fill with lettuce and scrambled eggs, top with a mixture of cooked shrimp, pickled ginger, scallion strips, and soy sauce

Bread for Charles
An English muffin base: top with mustard mayonnaise blended with chopped apples, gherkins, and anchovies; layer with batavia lettuce and cooked ham

Bread for Laurel
A sourdough sandwich: spread with cream cheese, fill with lettuce, tomatoes, and slices of hardboiled egg; top with capers, chives, and plenty of Parmesan

Bread for Gregory
A classic sandwich: fill with iceberg lettuce and slices of roast chicken in a yogurt dressing with curry powder, mango chutney, and Worcestershire sauce. Top with bean sprouts

Bread for Claudia
Ciabatta sandwich: spread with a paste of puréed baked beans and pesto. Fill with salami, sun-dried tomatoes, and arugula

Bread for Pedro
A piece of French bread: spread with a blend of green bell peppers, chili sauce, and garlic; fill with radicchio and tuna, top with grated cheese

Hot rice

When cooking rice, don't forget: 3/4 cup becomes 1 1/2 cups — plenty for two as a side.

When rice is being cooked, it drastically increases in volume, because the grains absorb the liquid. The ideal situation is reached when all the liquid is in the grains; the rice is flaky and full of flavor. It's really easy to achieve.

Use parboiled long grain rice and simply let it swell:

Place 3/4 cup rice and 1 2/3 cups cold liquid in a saucepan, bring to a boil, reduce the heat, and simmer gently, until all the liquid has been absorbed. This will take about 20 minutes. Leave the rice uncovered for a moment, stir with a fork, and that's it.

It's even easier to cook rice the Turkish way—and pilau rice sounds more interesting too:

Heat 2 tablespoons oil in a saucepan, add 3/4 cup rice and sauté until opaque, while stirring. Pour in 1 1/2 cups liquid, season to taste, cover, and simmer over a medium heat for 10 minutes. Resist the temptation to peek into the pan (the steam escapes!) or to stir (the rice will not end up flaky!!). Only at the very end are you allowed to look. If almost all the liquid has been absorbed, and the rice has formed holes on the surface (for the steam to escape), we can move to the next phase: Turn off the heat and leave the rice to stand covered or place in a warm oven (200°F) for 10 minutes. Now you can stir it. Serve a beautifully flaky and very tasty rice.

On page 51 you find out how the Greeks prepare pilau rice.

Our favorite comforter

Pasta

Spanish tallarín; Italian pasta; French nouille

Here's what it is
• In Italy: spaghetti and macaroni, rigatoni (short and hollow), penne (short, hollow and cut at an angle), tagliatelle, fettuccine, linguine, trenette (long, flat, thin to broad), farfalle (butterfly), ravioli (filled), tortellini (filled and twisted), and hundreds more
• In Asia: glass noodles (made from mung beans, for salads and soups), rice noodles (from very thin to tagliatelle size), Hokkien and Shanghai noodles (fresh wheat noodles, ideal for frying), somen, ramen, and udon noodles (mainly for Japanese soup dishes)
• In German-speaking countries: ribbon noodles, spaetzle, nockerl

Here's what it makes you
• strong and happy, but not fat
• want to eat more, can be habit-forming

Here's what it wants
• to boil, not to simmer
• to be eaten immediately
• lots of sauce
• no left-over hot water
• hot plates

Here's what it likes
• practically everything that's tasty—from a knob of butter to a slice of truffle
• sauces with tomatoes, cream, cheese, mushrooms, meat, or fish
• the aroma of garlic, Parmesan, basil, olive oil, and black pepper. Or scallions, ginger, coriander, soy sauce, and chilies.

Which variety of potato to choose for what?

There are people who can draw 37 different shapes of ravioli just like that and who order basmati rice directly from Karachi via the Internet. Well yes, but...the same people go to their supermarket and choose a potato to make a potato salad—and find they are making mashed potatoes instead. Well yes...

The right potato at the right time has more flavor and aroma than any pasta or any rice could ever have. Potatoes are one of the most interesting vegetables, but the varieties can be very different. Fortunately, in the U.S.A. potatoes are usually sold with a label indicating how they may best be used. And the most popular variety, Russell Burbank, is very versatile. You can safely use it for just about everything except salads, when a mainly "waxy" type that will remain firm when boiled should be in your saucepan.

Yes, we will
Discover and cook Asian noodles • cook spaghetti that doesn't stick together • make polenta with roast pork • use basmati rice • toss pancakes in the air • try sandwiches from all over the world • have a sandwich creation of the day • ALWAYS: baked potatoes, mushroom risotto, crispy pizza

No, we won't
Cut glass noodles for soups • cut spaghetti • have more cooking liquid than sauce with pasta • serve gnocchi with béchamel sauce • make risotto with milk rice • limit hot sandwiches to melted cheese • call pancakes "crêpes" • NEVER EVER: say ,"The main thing is to fill me up!"

Spaghetti alla bolognese
a.k.a. spaghetti with meat sauce

Serves 4 hungry people:

1 onion

1 carrot

2 celery stalks

1/4 pound bacon

2 tablespoons butter

3/4 pound ground beef (or add veal and/or pork)

1/2 cup red wine or stock

1 can tomatoes (14 ounces approx.)

1–4 small dried chilies

salt, freshly ground pepper

1 pound spaghetti

1 generous lump of Parmesan cheese

(will do for many more pasta dishes)

1 First prepare everything that has to go in the skillet: Peel the onion and carrot, wash the celery, and finely dice.

2 Place a large skillet on the stove and wait until it is hot. Fry the diced bacon over a medium heat until the fat has almost dissolved. Add the butter and stir in the vegetables.

3 Move the vegetables and the bacon to the side of the skillet to create space in the middle. Place the ground meat in the middle, divide it into small portions, using a spatula. Fry for 2–3 minutes, stirring constantly, until all the ground meat has turned into small crispy crumbs.

4 Pour in the wine or stock. Add the canned tomatoes with their juice, slightly mash the tomatoes, mix thoroughly. Chop the chilies and add. Season with 1 teaspoon salt and pepper. Gently simmer over a moderate heat for at least 15 minutes (1 hour may be even better), stirring occasionally.

5 Now it is time for the pasta: In a very large saucepan bring 5 quarts water to a boil, adding 2 tablespoons salt. Pour the spaghetti into the boiling water, stirring with a spoon to quickly immerse all the spaghetti.

6 Boil uncovered for 7–8 minutes, then fish out a strand and try. Spaghetti should never be too soft, but obviously not too hard either—just perfectly *al dente*. If the sauce has become too thick, add a little cooking liquid. Thoroughly drain the spaghetti in a colander.

7 Season the sauce to taste with salt and pepper. Transfer the spaghetti to soup plates and generously top with the sauce. Serve the Parmesan with a cheese grater—everybody will freshly grate it over their own plate of steaming spaghetti.

Time you need: 45 minutes
Goes well with: French bread, green salad, red wine—preferably Chianti
Calories per portion: 900

Fried Asian noodles
Just that little bit exotic

Serves 4 curious and hungry people:

1/2 pound Asian egg noodles

salt

1 pound chicken breast filets

1 bunch scallions

1 small piece fresh ginger

2 garlic cloves

1–2 small dried chilies

5–6 tablespoons neutral oil (e. g. canola oil)

3 tablespoons soy sauce

1–2 tablespoons lemon juice

1 Cook the noodles in 2 quarts boiling salted water for about 5 minutes (follow the instructions on the package). They must not be too soft, since they will be fried later. Thoroughly drain in a colander.

2 Cut the chicken into thin strips. Wash and trim the scallions, removing only the green parts that seem no longer fresh. Finely cut the scallions in either rings or strips. Peel the fresh ginger and the garlic and very finely chop. Finely crumble or chop the chilies; wash your hands.

3 Brush a large skillet or wok with 3–4 tablespoons oil and heat to get it really hot. Place the chicken in the skillet or wok, stirring vigorously and fry for only 1–2 minutes each side. Move to the side of the wok, pour new oil into the middle and fry the onions, ginger, garlic, and chilies.

4 Add the noodles with the remaining oil, stirring constantly. After about 1 minute pour over the soy sauce and lemon juice. It should sizzle and splutter and smell beautifully Asian. Now you need your chopsticks—don't use a fork!

Time you need: 30 minutes
Goes well with: green tea, jasmine tea, or beer
Calories per portion: 630

43

Spaghetti aglio olio
Costs nothing, very easy, very quick

Serves 4 spontaneously hungry people:

salt, 1 pound spaghetti

4 garlic cloves

5 tablespoons olive oil

freshly ground pepper

1 In a very large saucepan bring 5 quarts water to a boil, adding 2 tablespoons salt. Add the spaghetti and boil uncovered until *al dente* (try after 7–8 minutes!).

2 Peel the garlic and finely slice. Pour the olive oil into a large skillet and slowly heat—do not let it become sizzling hot! Gently fry the garlic in the hot oil.

3 Thoroughly drain the spaghetti in a colander and place in the skillet. Mix well with the garlic. Season to taste with salt and pepper.

Time you need: 20 minutes
Goes well with: arugula, Italian white wine, French bread
Calories per portion: 520

Spaghetti vongole
Impressive!
Two large saucepans needed!

Serves 4 gourmets:

salt, 1 pound spaghetti

2 pounds very small clams (shells on)

1 large onion

3–4 garlic cloves

2 small dried chilies

6 tablespoons olive oil

1/2 cup dry white wine

1 bunch parsley

freshly ground pepper

1 In a large saucepan bring 5 quarts water to a boil with 2 tablespoons salt. In the meantime, wash the clams, discarding all the open ones. Peel the onion and garlic. Halve the onion and cut into thin strips, chop the garlic. Chop or crumble the chilies.

2 In another large saucepan heat the olive oil. Add the onion, garlic and chili, stir, and cook for 2 minutes. Add the clams, pour in the wine, enjoy the aroma—and cover! Gently simmer for 10 minutes. Make sure your heat is moderate—the clams are not supposed to boil vigorously.

3 Now it is time for the spaghetti. Add to the boiling water and cook uncovered until *al dente* (try a strand to check after about 7–8 minutes!).

4 Wash the parsley and shake dry, finely chop. (The bigger the chopping knife, the better the result—try it out.) Uncover the saucepan containing the clams, discard all that are closed. Add salt, pepper, and parsley to the rest and stir—that's all. Drain the spaghetti and thoroughly mix with the clams—enjoy!

Time you need: 40 minutes
Goes well with: lots of fresh French bread for mopping up the juices
Calories per portion: 670

Basic Tip

Spaghetti always tastes wonderful — but it does not always need to be spaghetti. All of these sauces are just as delicious with tagliatelle or penne or rigatoni or fusilli or...

44

Spaghetti with tomato sugo
Perfect for unexpected guests

Serves 4 desperately hungry people:

1 onion, 2 garlic cloves

2–3 tablespoons olive oil

2 cans tomatoes (14 ounces each approx.)

salt, freshly ground pepper

1 pound spaghetti

1 large piece Parmesan cheese (will do for many more pasta dishes)

1 Peel and very finely chop the onion and the garlic. Heat the olive oil in a large skillet and gently fry the onion and garlic. Open the cans of tomatoes and with a knife cut up the tomatoes. Add the tomatoes and the tomato juice, season with salt and pepper. Simmer for 10 minutes or longer, stirring occasionally.

2 Meanwhile, in a very large saucepan bring 5 quarts water to a boil together with 2 tablespoons salt. Pour in the spaghetti and boil uncovered until *al dente* (try after about 7–8 minutes!).

3 Try the sauce—is there anything missing? Certainly pepper and salt. But if you like it hotter, add chili powder; fruitier, add

1 tablespoon balsamic vinegar; runnier, add 1 glass of red wine; healthier, add parsley...

4 Thoroughly drain the spaghetti and mix with the hot tomato sugo. Serve with fresh Parmesan to grate.

Time you need: 30 minutes
Goes well with: French bread, water, wine
Calories per portion: 590

Spaghetti with lemon cream and shrimp
Quick and excellent

Serves 4 hungry people with great expectations:

4 scallions, 1 teaspoon butter

salt, 1 pound spaghetti

1 cup heavy cream

1/2 cup vegetable stock

2–3 tablespoons lemon juice

freshly ground pepper

1/2 pound small, peeled, cooked shrimp

a few basil leaves

1 Wash and trim the scalions, remove outer green leaves. Cut in fine strips. Melt the butter in a large skillet and gently sauté the scallions.

2 In a very large saucepan bring 5 quarts water to a boil with 2 tablespoons salt. Add the spaghetti and cook uncovered until *al dente* (try after 7–8 minutes!).

3 Add the cream, vegetable stock, and lemon juice to the scallions and gently simmer, stirring occasionally. The liquid slowly evaporates leaving a deliciously creamy sauce. (If it curdles, this means the cream is no longer fresh.)

4 Try the sauce and season to taste with salt and pepper. At the very end, mix in the shrimp, just to heat not cook, to avoid them getting tough. Drain the spaghetti in a colander and instantly mix with the sauce. Garnish with basil leaves and serve immediately!

Time you need: 30 minutes
Goes well with: French bread and wine
Calories per portion: 670

Green lasagne
Definitely not for lazy cooks

Serves 4–6 fairly hungry people:

4 tablespoons butter

3 tablespoons flour

3 cups milk

1 bayleaf

1 small piece organic lemon zest

salt, freshly ground pepper

freshly grated nutmeg

1 onion

2 garlic cloves

4 tablespoons olive oil

1 pound ground beef (or mushrooms)

1 can tomatoes (14 ounces approx.)

1/2 cup red wine

2 tablespoons melted butter (for dish), a few knobs butter for topping finish

12 sheets green lasagne (precooked)

1/2 cup freshly grated Pecorino cheese

1 When you prepare a lasagne you learn to make one of the real basics of cooking—the most important of all sauces, the one even your great-grandmother could not live without: béchamel sauce!

Melt the butter over a very low heat, sprinkle in the flour, stirring vigorously with a spoon until it turns light yellow. Quickly pour in the milk and continue to stir. Add the bayleaf and the zest for a fresh aroma and gently simmer for 10 or 15 minutes, until the sauce slightly thickens. Keep an eye on it and stir occasionally, preferably using a whisk—but it can't really go wrong. Remove the zest and the bayleaf, and season to taste with salt, pepper, and nutmeg.

2 The second main ingredient for a classic lasagne is bolognese sauce. Usually it is prepared with ground meat, which you can, however, replace with mushrooms. First peel and finely chop the onion and garlic. Heat the olive oil in a large skillet and sauté the onion and garlic. Mix in the meat (or the cleaned and sliced mushrooms) and fry, stirring constantly. Add the canned tomatoes with the tomato juice and the red wine, while stirring. Season generously with salt and pepper, cover and simmer for 15–20 minutes, until the rest is ready.

3 Begin with preheating the oven to 400 °F (convection oven 350 °F without preheating). Look for a suitable dish. It should be rectangular and must be ovenproof—it can be made of ceramic, glass, or metal. Did you find one? Brush the inside of your dish with melted butter.

4 And now on to the creative part: All ingredients have to be layered into the dish until they are all used up. Start with a little béchamel sauce, place a few sheets of lasagne on top, followed by the bolognese sauce, and then again the lasagne. Repeat this—béchamel sauce, lasagne, bolognese sauce, lasagne—finishing up with a top layer of béchamel sauce.

5 The easy part: Transfer the lasagne to the center of the oven and relax for 30 minutes. Then sprinkle on the cheese and add a few knobs of butter and bake for another 10 minutes. The seductively crispy lasagne will amaze your guests!

Time you need: to be active for 1 hour, relax for 40 minutes
Goes well with: big mixed salad
Calories per portion (6): 810

Lasagne sheets are versatile: they can be filled, rolled, cut into different shapes and used for a variety of dishes that usually require home-made pasta dough. Here is an example:

Filled sauerkraut roulades

Fry 1/4 pound diced bacon and 1 chopped onion, add 1 1/2 pounds chopped sauerkraut and caraway seeds and braise for 5 minutes. Precook 12 sheets of lasagne for 5 minutes, drain on a kitchen towel. Mix the sauerkraut with chopped parsley and 5–6 tablespoons crème fraîche, season to taste with salt and pepper. Spread the mixture on the lasagne sheets, roll them up, and cut each sheet into two roulades.
Place the roulades in a saucepan, standing them up side-by-side, and add 1 cup stock. Cover and bake for 30 minutes (conventional oven 400 °F / convection oven 350 °F).

Cheese spaetzle
Really basic, really cheap, really tasty

Serves 4 very hungry people:

1/2 pound Swiss cheese

4 cups all-purpose flour

4 eggs, salt

2 onions

3 tablespoons butter

freshly ground pepper

1 It's best to start with grating the cheese—because you must not let a spaetzle wait when it comes out of the water.

2 In a bowl, mix the flour with the eggs, 1–2 teaspoons salt, and about 1 cup lukewarm water. Stir until the dough is smooth, but not as firm as pastry or as runny as batter. It should be sticky and only slowly drop off the spoon.

3 Boil 3 quarts water with 1 tablespoon salt in a large saucepan. Peel the onions and cut into thin rings. Melt the butter in a small frying pan and cook the onions over a medium heat until golden-brown. Keep warm. Preheat the oven to 400 °F (convection oven 350 °F) and place a large ovenproof dish in the oven.

4 By now the water should be boiling. Place a colander or spaetzle-maker over the pan and force the dough through it with a wooden spoon. Or press the dough flat on a floured board, and with a sharp knife, cut off small pieces of dough and drop them into the boiling water. There should be only one layer of spaetzle cooking at a time. They are done when they float back to the surface, which takes 3–5 minutes. Remove each layer of spaetzle with a slotted spoon, drain well and place directly in the hot dish in the oven. Pepper each layer and sprinkle with cheese. Place the onions and the butter on the top layer, increase the heat of the oven (480 °F / convection oven 425 °F) and bake for another 5 minutes. The spaetzle are sure to satisfy even the most enormous hunger.

Time you need: 1 hour
Goes well with: crispy lettuce salad
Calories per portion: 735

Risotto, just risotto
Always impressive, always comforting

How do the Italians do it—the whole world is in love with their food! They have put two of the best loved Basics on menus everywhere: spaghetti and risotto. Spaghetti is easy, but risotto requires dedication and care. And a spoon!

Serves 4 gourmets as an intermediate

course:

1 onion

4 tablespoons butter

1 1/2 cups Italian short-grain rice

1/2 cup white wine

1 quart hot meat or chicken stock

a generous pinch saffron (threads or powder)

1/4 cup freshly grated Parmesan cheese

(about 4–5 tablespoons)

salt, freshly ground pepper

1 Even if you feel you can't wait to stir that beautifully tempting risotto, you must start by peeling and finely dicing the onion. Melt 2 tablespoons of butter in a large skillet and sauté the onions until they become transparent.

2 It get's more exciting when it is time to pour the rice into the skillet. You need to stir it in the onion butter until it turns light and translucent—over a very, very gentle heat. To prevent it from browning, you should pour in the wine and a ladleful of hot stock right away, and keep stirring.

3 Obviously, the skillet will not be covered —because you are constantly stirring. There is, however, another reason: The liquid must not only be absorbed by the rice, it must also evaporate and be constantly replenished with new stock, which you add a ladleful at a time.

4 While stirring, the risotto cook will be ecstatic to see the moist, velvety texture of the rice—watching it turn into an almost devine paste. It will appear even more beautiful when the saffron, dissolved in the last ladleful of stock, adds a golden glow.

5 All in all, you have probably now been standing at the stove for 20–30 minutes without feeling bored in the slightest. The first spoonful is for the cook—to make sure that the beautifully soft rice still has a little bite to it—hooray!

6 Combine the rest of the butter and the freshly grated aromatic Parmesan cheese (do not use a package of grated Parmesan, please!) with the rice and season to taste with salt and pepper—basta!

Time you need: 40 minutes
Goes well with: a light, tangy white wine
Calories per portion: 390

Basic Tip

Once you have been bitten by the risotto bug, you might want to try out a new flavor every day. There is asparagus and pumpkin, for example. Or it could be fresh chanterelles or dried porcini, peas or fennel, cucumber or artichokes, ham or squid. The principle always remains the same: cook the ingredients in butter, stir in the rice, and continue as described above. There is one exception, though. Fish, shrimp, and other delicate ingredients that should not be simmered for a long time are mixed in at the very end. They only need to cook for a few minutes.

Paella
A feast for cooks

If you still haven't managed to bring back a paella pan from your vacation in Spain, you simply have to use the biggest skillet you can find.

Serves 6 hungry people:

6 small chicken legs

1 pound mussels and clams

6 jumbo shrimp in their shells

1/2 pound firm garlic sausage (chorizo)

1 red and 1 green bell pepper

1 pound beefsteak tomatoes

1 large onion

3 garlic cloves

5 cups chicken or meat stock

8 tablespoons olive oil

3/4 pound frozen peas

salt, freshly ground pepper

1 teaspoon sweet paprika

large pinch saffron (threads or powder)

2 1/2 cups short-grain rice (Spanish or Italian)

2 lemons

1 Lots of ingredients, and very little stress: Wash and pat dry the chicken legs, mussels, clams, and shrimp (discard open mussels and clams). Slice the garlic sausage.

2 Wash and halve the bell peppers. Seed and cut into strips. Wash and finely dice the tomatoes, removing the green stem ends. Peel and finely chop the onion and garlic.

3 Heat the stock in a large saucepan, add the mussels and clams and cook until the shells open (2–3 minutes). Remove from the stock, keep the stock warm. Discard any unopened mussels and clams.

4 Pour oil into the giant skillet and heat it. Fry the chicken legs on all sides over a high heat for about 15 minutes. Remove from the pan and season with salt and pepper. Now fry the jumbo shrimp, but only for about 1–2 minutes, until they turn nicely red. Remove from the pan.

5 Now stir the onions and garlic into the hot oil, add the bell pepper strips, tomatoes, and peas (still frozen). Season with salt, pepper, and paprika. Dissolve the saffron in the hot stock.

6 Almost forgotten—the rice! Mix it in well and immediately add the hot stock. Simmer for 15 minutes, until the rice has absorbed almost all of the liquid. After 5 minutes start preheating the oven to 360 °F (convection oven 325 °F without preheating).

7 Everything that has been put aside earlier —chicken legs, mussels, clams, shrimp, sausage—must now be nicely arranged on top of the rice. Cover with foil and place in the oven for about 30 minutes. That leaves you time to set the table, open the wine, cut the lemon in wedges—and look forward to eating! Olé!

Time you need: a good 2 hours
Goes well with: Spanish dry white wine
Calories per portion: 820

Nasi goreng
A hot use for left-overs

The Indonesians have really been ingenious with their national dish: nasi (cooked rice) can be prepared with a thousand and one different ingredients—vegetables, spices, fish, or meat—and it is always delicious and the best way to use up left-over bits of yesterday's rice dish (goreng!).

Serves 2 hungry people:

1 1/2 cups long-grain rice, salt

4 scallions

2 carrots

1/2 pound Chinese cabbage

1/4 pound bean sprouts

2 garlic cloves

1 piece fresh ginger

5 tablespoons oil

3 tablespoons soy sauce (preferably the sweet Indonesian Kecap manis)

1–2 teaspoons sambal paste (hot chili paste, available in different varieties)

1–2 tablespoons lemon juice

1 tablespoon tomato ketchup

4 eggs

freshly ground pepper

1 Wash the rice and place it in a saucepan. Add 3 cups water and salt, cover, and bring to a boil. Reduce the heat drastically and leave to swell (still covered) for 15–20 minutes. Remove from the heat and set aside, still covered.

2 Wash and trim the scallions, peel the carrots. Wash the Chinese cabbage, remove the stalk. Cut the vegetables in thin strips. Rinse the bean sprouts, drain. Peel the garlic and ginger and finely chop.

3 Heat 4 tablespoons of oil in a wok or large skillet. Add the garlic, ginger, and all the vegetables except for the bean sprouts and stir-fry for 2 minutes, using a spatula. Add the rice and continue to stir-fry for another 2 minutes. Season with soy sauce, sambal paste, lemon juice, and ketchup. Mix in the bean sprouts and continue to stir-fry for another 2–3 minutes.

4 Now comes the Indonesian challenge: Simultaneously heat the rest of the oil in a second skillet and fry 4 eggs. Season with salt and pepper. Transfer the rice onto plates and put the fried egg on top. By the way: The chopsticks shown are purely decorative!

Time you need: 45 minutes
Goes well with: cucumber slices, fried onions, shrimp toast
Calories per portion: 640

Pure pilau
Can't go wrong

Another ingenious method, which always works (the Greeks invented this one). One important thing: Add the rice to the boiling stock, cover, and do not stir!

Serves 4 hungry people as a side dish:

1 1/2 cups long-grain rice

1 onion

2–3 tablespoons butter

3 cups chicken stock

salt, freshly ground pepper

1/2 teaspoon grated lemon zest

1 Put the rice in a colander and wash under cold water, drain. Peel and finely chop the onion. Melt half the butter in a saucepan and sauté the onion until transparent. Add the stock and bring to a boil.

2 Only now add the rice. Season with salt, pepper, and lemon zest. Reduce the heat to the lowest possible level, cover, and wait for about 20 minutes—don't stir!

3 When the rice has absorbed all the liquid, remove from the heat. Place a dish towel between the pan and the lid and leave the rice to stand for 10 minutes. Loosen the rice with a fork, and fold in the rest of the butter. Perfect!

Time you need: 45 minutes
Goes well with: practically everything—from grilled fish to a vegetable medley
Calories per portion: 130

Pancakes
For filling, not stacking

These pancakes have to be one thing only and that is thin. Because you want to roll them up and put them straight in your mouth. Or you want to fill them with lots of lovely things, then put them in your mouth.

Serves 2 hungry people (or 4 sparrows):

1 1/4 cups all-purpose flour, 1/2 cup milk

4 eggs, 1 pinch salt

2 tablespoons shortening, oil, or clarified butter

1 Sift the flour into a bowl with a pinch of salt. Slowly beat in the eggs and the milk. The batter should be smooth and thick. Leave to stand for 20 minutes.

2 Lightly brush a skillet with oil and heat. When hot, reduce to a moderate heat. Pour in a small portion of the batter and thinly spread it evenly in the skillet.

3 When the pancake turns crispy, briefly shake the skillet to loosen it, then turn it using a spatula, and continue to cook.

4 Lightly brush the pan again with oil, pour in the next portion of batter, and cook as before. Each pancake only takes a few minutes, but by the time you have made the last one, the first one will be cold and wrinkled. It is therefore important to either eat the pancakes straight from the skillet or keep them warm in a preheated oven (350 °F/ convection oven 325 °F).

Time you need: 1 hour
Goes well with: lettuce, meat, or vegetable sauces
Tasty and quick: top the pancakes with cheese while they are still in the pan, roll, and let the cheese melt. Delicious also with compote, fruit salad or jam.
Calories per portion (4 pancakes): 270

Vegetable frittata
An Italian omelette

Serves 4 hungry people as an appetizer:

1/2 pound small, firm zucchini (or other vegetable)

1 small onion

2 garlic cloves

4 tablespoons olive oil

salt, freshly ground pepper

1 bunch chives

5 eggs

5 tablespoons milk

Potato tortilla
Olé!

Serves 4 hungry people as an appetizer:

2 big potatoes (3/4 pound)

1 onion

6–8 tablespoons olive oil

8 eggs

8 tablespoons milk

8 tablespoons heavy cream

salt, freshly ground pepper

3/4 pound frozen peas

1 bunch parsley

1 Wash and peel the potatoes. Chop the potatoes to the size of dice used for games (first cut into thick slices, then into thick strips, then dice). Peel and finely chop the onion.

2 Heat the oil in a skillet (which has a lid). Fry the potatoes over a medium heat for 10 minutes, turning occasionally. Add the onions and continue to fry for another 5 minutes.

3 Beat the eggs with the milk and the cream, season with salt and pepper. Wash the parsely and shake dry, finely chop, and mix in.

4 Pour the egg mixture over the potatoes and let it set over a moderate heat, until the bottom is firm. Slide the tortilla onto a plate and transfer it back into skillet upside down. Cover and continue to cook for another 5 minutes.

5 Serve immediately while warm, or let it cool down and cut it into bite size pieces to serve as tapas with a glass of sherry.

Time you need: 45 minutes
Goes well with: stuffed olives
Calories per portion: 430

1 Wash and trim the zucchini. First cut them into slices, then into thin sticks. Peel and finely chop the onion and garlic. Heat the olive oil in a skillet, mix in the zucchini, onion, and garlic and stir-fry. Season to taste with salt and pepper.

2 Wash and finely chop the chives. Beat the eggs with the milk, season to taste with salt and pepper. Mix in half of the chives. Pour the egg mixture over the zucchini, spreading it evenly. Let set over a low heat.

3 Slide the frittata onto a plate and transfer it back into the skillet upside down. Cover and continue to cook for another 5 minutes.

Time you need: 30 minutes
Goes well with: grated cheese, fresh tomato sauce, lettuce
Calories per portion: 210

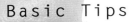

Basic Tips

Trick No. 1: Replace half the milk with mineral water to make the batter nice and light.
Trick No. 2: To turn the pancake, just toss it in the air and catch it again with the frying pan. Very cool!

Mashed potatoes
As good as they come

Are there still people around who have eaten real home-made mashed potatoes? Probably quite a few. And are there still people who know how to make them? Only very few. Well, here is the perfect recipe.

Serves 4 hungry people as a side dish
1 2/3 pounds potatoes
1 teaspoon salt
1 onion
1/2 stick butter
2/3–3/4 cup milk
freshly grated nutmeg

1 Wash and peel the potatoes. Halve medium-sized potatoes and quarter large ones. Place them in a saucepan with warm salted water, cover, and bring to a boil. Cook over a medium heat for at least 15 minutes.

2 Meanwhile, peel, halve, and thinly slice the onion. Melt the butter, add the onion, and brown over a medium heat. Bring the milk to a boil.

3 Drain the potatoes and leave them to stand uncovered for 1 minute. Mash the potato pieces or push them through a potato ricer back into the saucepan.

4 Pour over the hot milk and combine well, first using a spoon and then a whisk to make sure the mashed potatoes will be light. Grate the nutmeg over the potatoes.

5 Now it's up to you: Do you want to mix the butter and the onions with the mashed potatoes, or do you want to put them on top? We recommend pouring the butter through a strainer, blending it in, and spreading the onions over the top. There is no better way!

Time you need: 30 minutes
Goes well with: roast meat, fried fish
Calories per portion: 250

54

Basic Tip

Delicious, but cold – that's the eternal problem with mashed potatoes. It is therefore vital that all the ingredients are as hot as possible when they are mixed together. Whisk the mashed potatoes over a very gentle heat: They'll stay hot, and also lovely and light. To keep them warm, place the saucepan on top of another (roughly the same size) full of boiling water.

Potatoes boiled in their skins
Really Basic, really good

Serves 4 hungry people:

2 1/2 pounds potatoes, all roughly

the same size

salt

2 1/4 cups sour cream

a few tablespoons milk

freshly ground pepper

1 bunch chives (or other fresh herbs)

1 piece horseradish (about 2 inches long)

1 1/2 sticks fresh butter

1 Wash and thoroughly brush the potatoes under running water, so that the skins can be eaten.

2 Place in a saucepan, just cover with water, add 1 teaspoon of salt. Cover and cook over a moderate heat for about 30 minutes. Check with a fork if the potatoes are done.

3 Meanwhile, combine the sour cream with milk, salt, and pepper. Wash and chop the herbs and add. Wash, peel, and coarsely grate the horseradish.

4 Drain the potatoes, and briefly set aside.

5 Cover with a cloth to prevent them from cooling down. Serve the potatoes nice and hot, still in their skins. Serve with the sour cream, horseradish, butter, and salt.

Time you need: 45 minutes
Goes also well with: tuna salad, smoked salmon, frankfurters—and the sauces and dips from page 88 onward (for example, green sauce, tzatziki, tuna dip, Provençal vegetable sauce)
Calories per portion: 630

Baked potatoes
No stress at all

Serves 4 hungry people:

8 big potatoes (each weighing 5–8 ounces)

caraway or cilantro seeds

cracked black pepper

dried herbs, such as majoram, thyme,

oregano, rosemary

1 Preheat the oven to 450°F / convection oven 400°F without preheating. Put a baking rack in the middle of the oven.

2 Wash the potatoes, prick them with a fork and wrap them in foil, adding the caraway or cilantro, pepper and herbs.

3 Place the potatoes on the tray and cook for about 1 hour (depending on size).

Time you need: 1 hour 15 minutes
Goes well with: salt and fresh butter, sour cream, cream cheese with herbs, steak and salad
Calories per portion: 210

Fried potatoes
Old-time favorite!

First version!

Serves 4 hungry people as a side dish:

2 pounds potatoes

4–6 tablespoons clarified butter or canola oil

salt, freshly ground pepper

1 Wash the potatoes, place in a saucepan, cover with salted water, and cook. Drain and let cool down (overnight is fine). Peel and cut into thin slices.

2 Heat half of the fat in a skillet (do not use a nonstick pan) and fry the potato slices side-by-side over a medium heat for 10 minutes, without turning. Season with salt and pepper, turn, and fry another 5 – 8 minutes until crispy.

Second version!

2 pounds potatoes (same as before)

6 tablespoons olive oil

2 tablespoons butter

salt, freshly ground pepper

1 Wash, peel, and dice the potatoes. Heat the oil in a skillet pan with a lid. Add the potatoes, fry, and turn.

2 Cover and fry over a medium heat for 10–15 minutes, until golden-brown. Remove the lid, add the butter and fry for another 5–10 minutes, turning occasionally. Season to taste with salt and pepper.

Time you need:
No. 1: 1 hour (plus cooling down time)
No. 2: 40 minutes
Goes well with: practically everything from fried eggs to roast pork
Calories per portion:
No. 1: 210
No. 2: 270

Potato gratin
Looks lovely

Serves 4 hungry people as a side dish

1/2 cup heavy cream

1/2 cup milk

1 pound potatoes

1 tablespoon butter for the ovenproof dish and the extra knobs

salt, freshly ground pepper

freshly grated nutmeg

1/2 cup grated Swiss cheese

1 Mix the heavy cream with the milk. Wash and peel the potatoes. Cut the potatoes into thin slices. Preheat the oven to 350 °F (convection oven 325 °F without preheating).

2 Butter an ovenproof dish and layer with overlapping potato slices. Season each layer with salt, pepper, and a little nutmeg. Add the cream mixture, sprinkle with cheese, and cover with knobs of butter. Cook in the oven for 50 minutes, until the potatoes are soft and golden-brown.

Time you need: 1 hour
Goes well with: roast duck, roast beef, or just a delicious salad
Calories per portion: 245

57

Dumplings
The real thing

Serves 4 hungry people as a side dish:

2 pounds potatoes

1–1 1/2 cups all-purpose flour

salt

freshly grated nutmeg

2 medium eggs

2–3 tablespoons butter

4 tablespoons dry breadcrumbs

1 If you have a potato ricer, you can go straight to Step No. 2, if you don't, you have to continue reading. Wash the potatoes, place them in a saucepan, cover with salted water, and cook. Drain and let cool down overnight. Peel and grate the potatoes (continue with No. 3).

2 For those who own a potato ricer: Wash the potatoes, place in a saucepan, cover with salted water, and cook. Drain, let cool down briefly, and peel immediately. Push through a potato ricer, making sure that there are no lumps.

3 Sprinkle about two-thirds of the flour over the potatoes, season to taste with salt and nutmeg. Mix in the flour, using your fingers. In a bowl beat the eggs with a fork

and fold in the potato mixture. Then quickly knead it into a smooth dough. If it doesn't stick together, add more flour. Make sure not to knead too vigorously since the dough must not be too soft.

4 Coat your hands with flour, and divide the dough into small portions, depending on the size of dumpling you want. Roll each portion into a ball. In a very large saucepan bring 5 quarts water to a boil.

5 Drop the dumplings into the boiling water, cover, and bring to a boil again. Simmer for 10–20 minutes (depending on the size) until the dumplings float back to the surface.

6 Melt the butter in a small skillet, mix in the breadcrumbs and brown. Remove the dumplings with a skimming ladle and drain. Pour over the breadcrumbs.

Time you need: 1 hour 15 minutes
Goes well with: everything with lots of sauce or gravy—meat, poultry, vegetables, mushrooms
Calories per portion: 400

Basic Tips

Two suggestions for filled dumplings:

Finely dice white bread, and briefly fry in butter. Or cut open plums, and replace the pit with a sugar lump. To place the filling right in the middle of the dumpling, flatten the portions of dough in your hands, put the bread or the plum in the center, and roll into a perfect ball.

A German classic: potato pancakes

Peel raw potatoes and grate, but not too finely. Place in a dish towel, and briefly press to remove excess liquid. Season with salt and pepper, and, using a spoon, place small portions into a skillet with hot clarified butter. Flatten with the spoon and fry until crispy. Serve the potato pancakes with apple sauce or sour cream.

Gnocchi and malfatti
Not an Italian gangster duo, but something superyummy!

Gnocchi are little potato dumplings—and that's why the dough is prepared in the same way as in the recipe on the left. But instead of a ball, form a long roll, cut the dough roll into small pieces, and press each piece with a fork to add little grooves. Now they are ready to be boiled! Drain and briefly toss in hot butter and sage leaves (photo at the top).
Malfatti means: badly done! But in reality they taste every bit as delicious as gnocchi (photo in the center).

Serves 4 hungry fans of Italian food:

1 tablespoon butter

3/4 pound frozen spinach (defrosted)

1/4 pound ricotta (Italian cream cheese)

1/2 cup freshly grated Parmesan cheese

2 eggs

1 egg yolk

salt, freshly ground pepper

freshly grated nutmeg

1 cup all-purpose flour

1 Butter an ovenproof dish. Finely chop the defrosted spinach and place in a bowl. Add the ricotta, half of the Parmesan, the eggs and egg yolk, and combine. Season to taste with salt, pepper, and nutmeg. Slowly add the flour; mix, using a hand-held blender, until the batter is smooth.

2 In a large saucepan bring 3 quarts salted water to a boil. Preheat the oven to 350 °F (convection oven 325 °F). Start forming the dumplings when the water boils. With a tablespoon, take a small portion of dough, flatten with another tablespoon and drop into the boiling water.

3 Simmer for a few minutes, until the dumplings float back to the surface. Remove with a slotted spoon, drain, and transfer to the ovenproof dish. Sprinkle with the remaining cheese, and bake in the oven for 5 minutes.

Time you need: 1 hour
Goes well with: dry white wine,
French bread, salad
Calories per portion: 420

French fries
From scratch—not as easy as you thought

Serves 4 hungry people anywhere, anytime:

1 1/2 pounds potatoes, salt

4 1/4 cups shortening, oil, or clarified butter

1 Wash, peel, and cut the potatoes into sticks. Wash again under running cold water and pat dry.

2 Thoroughly heat a large amount of fat in a very large saucepan (or use an electric deep fryer—safer). Test by frying a lump of bread—it must sizzle immediately.

3 Important: Prefry the potato sticks in small portions for 2–3 minutes, remove them when they turn yellow, drain. If you put all the potato sticks in at the same time, the fat cools down too quickly and is absorbed by the potatoes.

4 Place the prefried potato sticks back in the oil—this time they can all go in at the same time. Fry for 4–5 minutes until crispy, drain well, season with salt, enjoy.

Time you need: 45 minutes
Goes well with: doesn't really need anything
Calories per portion: 440

Baking a pizza
Child's play

Some rumors really are persistent, like the one about yeast dough: It's complicated, takes for ever, and often goes wrong. Not at all true!

Serves 4 hungry people:
The pizza dough:

1 1/2 cups all-purpose flour

1 pinch salt

4 tablespoons olive oil

1 envelope active dry yeast or 1 cube compressed cake yeast

fat for greasing the oven tray

The tomato sauce:

1 onion

2 garlic cloves

1 tablespoon olive oil

2 pounds plum tomatoes (or 1 big can peeled tomatoes, 28 ounces approx.)

salt, freshly ground pepper

The toppings:
mozzarella slices, basil

olives, anchovies, capers

ham, artichokes (from a jar)

fresh mushrooms, salami, pepperoni

tuna, bell peppers, onions,

goat's cheese, arugula, nuts...

1–2 tablespoons olive oil for drizzling

1 It could not be easier: In a bowl mix the flour with the salt and the oil. Dissolve the fresh yeast in 1/2 cup lukewarm water, stir until smooth and combine with the flour (dry yeast can be mixed with the flour before adding oil and lukewarm water). Knead into a workable dough, using your hands or the dough hooks of a hand-held blender. Cover the bowl with a cloth and leave to rise for about 45 minutes, until the volume of the dough has doubled. Finished!

2 Meanwhile prepare the tomato sauce and get the toppings ready.

3 Peel and finely chop the onion and garlic. Fry in hot olive oil. Chop the tomatoes and mix in (canned tomatoes still have to be chopped). Simmer the sauce over a medium heat uncovered, until smooth. Season to taste with salt and pepper.

4 Preheat the oven to 480 °F (convection oven 425 °F). Grease a cookie sheet. Place the dough on a floured surface and thoroughly knead again. Roll out to fit the oven tray, put the dough on the tray, forming a rim on the edges.

5 Spread the tomato sauce onto the dough—and let everybody put their own favorite toppings on. Sprinkle with a little olive oil and bake for 15–20 minutes.

Time you need: 1 hour 30 minutes
Goes well with: Italian red wine
Calories per portion: 410

Ham and cheese quiche
Ideal freezer food for emergencies

Serves 4–6 hungry people:
2 1/2 cups all-purpose flour
1/2 teaspoon salt
1 stick cold butter
1/4 pound cooked ham
1/4 pound dry-cured ham (need not be the most expensive one)
1 onion
2 garlic cloves
1 1/2 cups hard cheese (i.e. Swiss, mild cheddar...)
1 cup heavy cream
4 eggs
freshly ground pepper
1 bunch chives or parsley

1 Sift the flour into a mound, add salt, and make a well in the middle. Pour in 2–3 tablespoons of very cold water. Dice the butter and place on the edge of the flour. With a big knife chop through the mixture until it has the consistency of breadcrumbs. Knead to a soft dough, roll into a ball, wrap in foil, and put in the fridge for 30 minutes.

2 This leaves you time to cut the ham into strips, peel and chop the onion and garlic, and grate the cheese. There is even time to combine the heavy cream, the eggs, the pepper, and finely chop the herbs.

3 Now don't forget to preheat the oven to 425 °F (convection oven 400 °F without preheating).

4 On a lightly floured surface roll out the dough to form a circle and place it in pie pan (11–12 inches); cut off the excess dough.

5 Mix the ham with the onion, garlic, and herbs and spread on the dough. Stir the cheese into the egg mixture and pour over. Bake the quiche for about 40 minutes until golden-brown. Cover with foil after about 20 minutes (shiny side on the quiche) to prevent it from turning too dark.

Time you need: to be active for 1 hour
baking 40 minutes
Goes well with: green salad
Calories per portion: (6): 685

Bruschetta
Good tomatoes + good
oil = good bruschetta

Serves 4 hungry people when they arrive:

4 ripe tomatoes

8 basil leaves

4 big slices of bread (Italian white bread
or sourdough loaf)

4 garlic cloves

8 tablespoons best olive oil

salt, freshly ground pepper

1 Wash the tomatoes and remove the green
stem ends. Very finely dice the tomatoes.
Cut the basil into fine strips.

2 Halve the bread slices and toast, either
in a toaster, under a broiler, or in the oven.

3 Peel and halve the garlic cloves and
rub on the toasted bread. Sprinkle about
1 tablespoon olive oil on each slice. Spread
the tomatoes on the bread, season to taste
with salt and pepper. Sprinkle with the basil.

Time you need: 20 minutes
Goes well with: prosecco or white wine
Calories per portion: 275

Crostini with olive paste
Has to be tried!

The world's most wonderful olive paste—
unfortunately, we did not invent it...

Serves 4 hungry apéritif drinkers:

1/4 pound black pitted olives

1 tablespoon capers

1 tablespoon pine nuts

2 tablespoons tomato purée

2 tablespoons olive oil

1 tablespoon balsamic vinegar

freshly ground pepper

12 thin slices French bread, Italian white
bread, ciabatta, or toast

1 Purée the pine nuts, tomato purée, and
oil, using a blender. Season with balsamic
vinegar and pepper (you don't need salt as
the olives are already quite salty).

2 Toast the bread slices, spread with the
olive paste and eat immediately.

Time you need: 10 minutes
Goes well with: any apéritif
Calories per portion: 235

Olga's slices
Impressive!

Olga always serves these slices of bread
when there is something to celebrate. And
Olga being a real Russian, we tend to eat
them quite often.

For 4 hungry people as prelude:

1 cup crème fraîche

2/3 cup sour cream

1 French bread

1 bunch chives

3 tablespoons black caviar (the real thing
from sturgeon, extremely expensive or the
substitute, though black, from lumpfish)

3 tablespoons red caviar (salmon roe)

1 Mix the crème fraîche with the sour
cream. Thinly slice the French bread. Wash
and finely chop the chives.

2 Thickly spread the cream on the bread,
top with black and red caviar and garnish
with chives.

Time you need: 15 minutes
Goes well with: champagne, of course,
or vodka served in tiny cups
Calories per portion: 540

P—Croissants
It's party time!

"P" for puff pastry and party—and full of ideas for delicious fillings. Simply make some more when more people arrive.

Serves 4 curious and hungry people:

4 sheets frozen puff pastry (about 3/4 pound)

salt, freshly ground pepper

1 egg

Some ideas for fillings:

1/4 pound mushrooms

1 tablespoon lemon juice

1/2 cup grated Swiss cheese

2 tablespoons chopped parsley

or:

1/2 pound cooked ham

1/2 cup grated Swiss cheese

1–2 tablespoons capers

2–3 tablespoons crème fraîche

sweet paprika powder

1 Place the sheets of puff pastry next to each other, letting them start to thaw. Roll into squares and cut diagonally into triangles. Preheat the oven to 360° F (convection oven 325 °F).

2 Clean and thinly slice or dice the mushrooms, sprinkle with lemon juice. Season with salt and pepper. Mix with the grated cheese and the chopped parsley.

3 Or cut the ham into fine strips and mix with the cheese, the capers, and the crème fraîche. Season to taste with pepper and paprika.

4 Separate the egg and brush the edges of the triangles with egg white (to make the croissants stick together). Spread the filling on the triangles and roll them into croissants. Beat the egg yolk; brush onto the croissants. Prick with a fork for the steam to escape.

5 Rinse a cookie sheet under cold water, place the croissants on it, and put in the center of the oven. After about 30 minutes they look temptingly delicious—and taste exactly like that.

Time you need: 50 minutes
Goes well with: salad
Calories per portion:
1. (mushroom) 360
2. (ham) 430

Oven-baked French bread
Nice and easy

Serves 4 hungry people as a snack:

2 garlic cloves

a few fresh basil leaves

4 tablespoons soft butter

3/4 pound mozzarella

4 medium-sized tomatoes

1 French bread

salt, freshly ground pepper

1 Preheat the oven to 400 °F (convection oven 360 °F). Peel and finely chop the garlic. Cut the basil into fine strips. Combine both with the soft butter. Slice the mozzarella and the washed tomatoes.

2 Make deep cuts into the French bread at intervals of about 3/4 inch, but do not cut through. Spread the butter mixture on the cuts in the bread and fill each cut with one slice of mozzarella and one slice of tomato. Bake in the hot oven for 15 minutes.

Time you need: 30 minutes
Goes well with: a glass of dry red wine
Calories per portion: 490

63

Salad
& so

s
ups

To make a good salad, you need an eye for detail. You'll make sure that the leaves are bite-size, that the tomato slices are not chilled, that the dressing and the ingredients make a perfect match. And when it comes to putting it all together—it must happen early enough for the salad to soak up the flavor, but late enough for it not to turn into a very limp affair.

If you can cook good soups, you can see the essential. From the very beginning you have to think about the outcome in the end and what has to be added and placed in the saucepan at what stage.

If you can see the essential and have an eye for detail, you really can cook.

People who make bad salads and soups, simply can't cook. Sorry to be so direct, but it is a fact.

And it's also a fact that it is easy to make good soups and salads.

And if you can make good soups and salads...

A favorite ingredient

The onion

Spanish cebolla; French
oignon; Italian cipolla

Here's what it is
• the ordinary onion in its brown skin can be
small and strong or large and mild
• the aromatic white onion
• the mildly aromatic red onion
• the shallot, both delicate and strong
• the refreshing scallion

Here's what it has
• 30 calories per 1/2 cup
• 7g carbohydrate
• hardly any protein and fat
• potassium and vitamin C

Here's what it does
• blows right through your respiratory tracts
• gets the digestion going
• cleans the blood
• moves to tears

Here's what it wants
• to be stored in a cool, completely dark, and
absolutely dry place
• to be kept completely on its own—
if not, everything will taste of it
• to be chopped freshly—
if not, it will go bitter
• to be sautéd before being cooked—
if not, it will never become soft
• not to hang around too long in a salad—
if it goes off, it will spoil everything

Here's what it likes
• to be fried—and become strong and crispy
• to be sautéd gently—and become sweet
and juicy
• powerful companions that can compete
with it—something tasty, hot, sour, fat,
smoked, fried
• sweet and creamy contrasts
• nothing half-cooked

Stock

A good stock
is a solid base.

As a versatile base, vegetable stock is best—
it is neutral in taste and easy to prepare.
Simply choose some of your favorite
vegetables, wash, clean, and trim, and place
in a saucepan. Add your favorite herbs and
spices and a pinch of salt. Cover with water,
gently bring to a boil, and simmer for
30–60 minutes, depending on the vegetables.
Delicate herbs with their stems are added
for the last 15 minutes only. Pass the stock
through a strainer and season to taste.
Clever: You can use vegetable leftovers
for the stock.

Ideal vegetables:
onions, tomatoes (for the basic taste and
color); leek, celery, carrots, and other root
vegetables; mushrooms, peppers, fennel (to
add a distinctive flavor); cauliflower, broccoli.

Ideal spices and herbs
(do not chop):
pepper, nutmeg, juniper berries, cloves; bay
leaves, rosemary, thyme, savory; chives,
parsley, tarragon, basil (at the end); ginger,
cinnamon, fennel, saffron, caraway seeds
for special dishes.

To infuse or not to infuse

What is worse than a pasta salad that was only allowed to infuse for 15 minutes?
Or lettuce that has been soaking in its dressing for 15 minutes ?
Here are the ideal infusing times for salads

1 minute	delicate lettuce (batavia, bibb lettuce, lamb's lettuce, arugula etc.), best freshly dressed
up to 5 minutes	firm lettuce (Chinese cabbage, radicchio, Belgian endive, romaine, chicory, frisée etc.)
15 minutes	tomato salad, warm potato salad
half a day	pasta salad, potato salad
overnight	herring salad
whole day	rice salad

Vinegar

How do you make vinegar? Easy: Open a bottle of wine and forget about it.

It'll turn vinegary. Because there are plenty of bacteria in the air eager to turn alcohol, if left exposed to air, into acetic acid or vinegar. The vinegar will taste of the original alcohol and will be named after it. Spirit or distilled vinegar, for example, is strong and tastes unpleasant, as its base is a rather flavorless alcohol distilled from sugar beets or potatoes. Wine vinegar can be excellent, if a fine wine was used—and if the producers did not just open the bottle and leave it. A good wine vinegar is made in the slow traditional way in oak barrels. The production of balsamic vinegar certainly requires expertise: It is fermented twice and left to mature for 10 to 30 years. It also requires very fine grape juice.

Other types of vinegars: sherry vinegar, cider vinegar, rasberry or other fruit vinegar, tarragon or other herb vinegar, malt vinegar (very British), beer vinegar (very Bavarian), rice vinegar (very Asian). Vinegar concentrate is best left in the cleaning cupboard.

Oil

How do you make oil? By pressing plants.

This even applies to mineral oil: The earth pressed it out of stone-age ferns. Edible oil is extracted from oily fruits or seeds—under high pressure, producing heat. In the end, a solvent is added to help squeeze out the last drop. When the solvent and other cloudy ballast have been filtered out again, you are left with refined oil. You can use it for frying, but it has absolutely no taste. It is quite good in salads, however, since it transmits flavor well. Cold-pressed oils have a strong aroma. They are extracted at a maximum temperature of 140 °F, with no solvent added. Cold-pressed oil is not refined and therefore preserves its flavor, which can be quite strong and very distinctive—if in doubt, try first! Olive oil is always pressed cold, and "virgin" means it does not undergo chemical treatment.

Other major oils: sunflower oil, corn oil and canola oil (usually refined, often blended to become plant or salad oil); pumpkin seed oil, nut oil, sesame oil (great aroma, often too strong on its own).

Salt

Salt always comes from the sea. This really is true.

Rock salt is mined from ancient salt deposits beneath the earth. Once, this was the sea, but the water evaporated. The salt was left, and another rock stratum built on it. Today, the salt reappears, usually dissolved in water—nature brings it to the surface again. It does this either on its own or with the help of pipes and pumps. Again, this water evaporates—but this time under pressure and steam. With sea salt, you do not need to take a detour of millions of years and rock strata. It is simply harvested. Sea water is pumped into shallow pans and starts to evaporate, leaving the salt to be extracted. For human consumption, this salt needs to be washed several times. Even so, the end product does not just taste salty, it tastes of the sea. If it is iodized, it'll help an under-active thyroid to function. Other additives, however, like herbs and vitamins, are better and fresher when obtained from other sources. Sea salt comes in fine or large crystals and always contains vital trace minerals. In food preparation salt is used for seasoning and as a preservative.

Yes, we will

Not always just vinegar, oil and salt: lemon dressing, cream cheese dressing or soy sauce • a well-stocked vinegar & oil bar • fresh herbs • enough stock in the freezer • Parmesan cheese on salads and soups • warm soup bowls • serving bowls instead of saucepans on the table • vegetable stew with curry and coconut milk • ALWAYS: balsamic vinegar with lettuce, nutmeg in bouillon

No, we won't

Leave water on lettuce and in dressing • keep old oil on the salad bar • use dried parsley and chives • put rosemary, thyme or oregano in the dressing • use alcohol in the dressing • make delicious soup but not enough for seconds • just cream, no solid pieces in soup • serve stew in espresso cups • noodles in creamy soups • NEVER EVER: oily salads, lukewarm soups

Lamb's lettuce with bacon and fried mushrooms
Only tell your very best friends about the mushroom trick!

Serves 4 hungry people as an appetizer:

1/3 pound bacon

1/2 pound lamb's lettuce

1/2 pound mushrooms

2 tablespoons canola oil to fry the mushrooms

salt, freshly ground pepper

1 dash dry white wine (or sherry or cognac or balsamic vinegar)

1–2 tablespoons red wine vinegar

2–3 tablespoons sunflower oil

1 Finely dice the bacon, place in a skillet and fry without oil over a medium heat until crispy.

2 Thoroughly wash the lamb's lettuce, 2–3 times. Remove the root ends, drain in a colander.

3 And now to the mushroom trick (works with all varieties): Clean the mushrooms—with paper towels for example—but do not wash. Trim and cut in halves or quarters. Heat 2 tablespoons oil in a big lidded skillet over a high heat. Briefly fry the mushrooms, season to taste with salt and pepper. Pour in a generous measure of wine and cover immediately. Wait 1 minute and the mushrooms are ready, giving off a beautiful aroma.

4 Whisk the vinegar with the oil, season to taste with salt and pepper. Spread the mushrooms with their juices over the lettuce, sprinkle with bacon, and add the vinaigrette. Serve immediately.

Time you need: 30 minutes
Goes well with: fresh bread
Calories per portion: 330

Caesar's salad
A restaurant favorite

Serves 4 hungry people as an appetizer:

1 big romaine lettuce

1/4 pound bacon

2 slices toast

3 tablespoons sunflower oil

2 garlic cloves

2 very fresh (!) eggs

3–4 tablespoons lemon juice

1/2 cup olive oil

2–3 teaspoons Worcestershire sauce

salt, freshly ground pepper

2 anchovy filets

1 small piece Parmesan cheese (2 ounces)

1 Clean the lettuce, wash thoroughly and drain in a colander.

2 Cut the bacon into strips and fry over a medium heat until crispy. Dice the toast. Remove the bacon from the skillet, add the oil, and fry the bread over a medium heat until it turns into crispy croûtons. Peel and finely chop the garlic and fry briefly together with the croutons.

3 Place the eggs in boiling water for 1 minute (not longer!). Rinse under cold water, crack the eggs open, and transfer the liquid content to a bowl, using a spoon. Combine with lemon juice, olive oil, and Worcestershire sauce. Season to taste with salt and pepper.

4 Cut the lettuce leaves crosswise into 3/4 inch wide strips, pour over the sauce. Rinse the anchovies, pat dry, and chop. Sprinkle the anchovies, the bacon, and the croûtons over the lettuce. Grate the Parmesan cheese over the top.

Time you need: 30 minutes
Goes well with: fresh white bread
Calories per portion: 450

Arugula
Very tasty & a little different

Rucola (Italian), Rauke (German), roquette (French)—once an Italian speciality, now to be found in every supermarket. Ideal for guests and for singles, as it is sold in very small quantities.

Serves 4 gourmets as an appetizer:

3/4 pound arugula

2 tablespoons balsamic vinegar

salt, freshly ground pepper

4 tablespoons good olive oil

10 sun-dried tomatoes in oil

1–2 tablespoons capers

2 slices white bread

1 garlic clove

1 Remove the hard stems from the arugula, rinse, and drain in a colander. Combine the balsamic vinegar, salt, pepper, and olive oil.

2 Take the tomatoes out of the oil and cut in strips. Dice the bread. Heat 1–2 tablespoons of the oil that the tomatoes were preserved in and fry the bread over a medium heat until crispy. Peel the garlic, push through a garlic press and add to the skillet.

3 Mix the arugula with the dressing, sprinkle with tomatoes, capers, and croûtons. That's it!

Time you need: 25 minutes
Goes well with: a light dry white wine, Italian white bread, olive ciabatta, or other interesting white bread
Calories per portion: 150

Variations:

With cheese and nuts
Instead of the tomatoes and bread, use 2 tablespoons pine nuts (briefly toast without oil in a skillet—delicious!). Sprinkle with 2 tablespoons freshly grated Parmesan cheese, and add the dressing.

With mushrooms and ham
Clean and trim 1/3 pound fresh mushrooms, thinly slice and sprinkle with 1 tablespoon lemon juice. Cut 4–6 slices of Parma ham into thin strips, dice a ball of mozzarella. Spread over the arugula, season to taste with salt and freshly ground pepper, and pour over the dressing.

With avocado and shrimp
Cut 1 ripe but not mushy avocado lengthwise, twist the halves against each other, and remove the pit. Peel and cut crosswise into thin slices. Sprinkle with 1–2 tablespoons lemon juice. Rinse 1/3 pound small peeled shrimp and drain well. Wash and halve 1/4 pound cherry tomatoes. Spread the avocado, shrimp, and tomatoes over the arugula, and drizzle with the dressing.

Vinaigrette
Really basic

A real classic—not only for a great variety of salads, but also for marinading meat and fish, for artichokes, or for barbecues. Depending on the vinegar, the oil, and the mustard, the vinaigrette will vary—try and find your favorite version.

To dress a salad for 4 people:

1 teaspoon mustard (try Dijon mustard!)

2–3 tablespoons wine vinegar (white or red)

salt, freshly ground pepper

6 tablespoons oil (sunflower oil, olive oil, nut oil—solo or in combination)

1 In a bowl combine the mustard, vinegar, salt, and pepper. Slowly pour in the oil and thoroughly whisk into a slightly creamy sauce. Season to taste—voilà!

Time you need: 2 minutes
Goes well with: any lettuce or mixed salad
Calories per portion: 110

Variations:

All variations are based on the recipe on the left.

Tomato vinaigrette
Immerse 1 tomato in a bowl of boiling water for 30 seconds, then drop in cold water for 1 minute, until cool enough to peel off the skin. Very finely dice the tomato and mix with the vinaigrette. Delicious with cold meat, warm lentils, sliced mozzarella.

Herb vinaigrette
Wash and very finely chop 1 bunch of fresh herbs and mix with the vinaigrette just before serving. Parsley is ideal for artichokes, chives for warm asparagus, dill for cucumber salad. You can also use the dressing to marinade steamed fish filets.

Yogurt dressing
Makes you fit for fun

Enough for 4:

2/3 cup yogurt

2 tablespoons lemon juice or white wine vinegar

1 tablespoons sunflower oil

salt, freshly ground pepper

1 bunch herbs (e.g. chives, dill, basil)

1 Combine the yogurt with the lemon juice or vinegar and the oil. Season to taste with salt and pepper.

2 Wash and finely chop the herbs. Mix in and season to taste again.

Time you need: 8 minutes
Goes well with: lettuce, tomatoes, cucumber or pasta salad, grilled vegetables
Calories per portion: 45

Cheese dressing
From very strong to very mild

Each is enough for 4:

2 ounces roquefort without rind

1/4 cup heavy cream

1–2 tablespoons white wine vinegar

freshly ground pepper

2 tablespoons sunflower oil

or:

2 ounces cream cheese, 1/4 cup yogurt

1–2 tablespoons lemon juice

salt, freshly ground pepper

1 tablespoon sunflower oil

1 For those who like strong flavors:
Mash the roquefort with a fork, and mix well
with the cream. Add the vinegar, a little pepper
and whisk in the oil.

2 For the milder dressing: Combine the
cream cheese with the yogurt and lemon
juice, a little salt and pepper. Whisk in the oil.

Time you need: 5–10 minutes
Goes well with: blue cheese dressing with
spinach, romaine lettuce, or chicory
cream cheese dressing with grated carrots,
bean sprouts, radishes, watercress
Calories per portion: 510 (1), 260 (2)

Lemon dressing
A Mediterranean basic

Enough for 4:

1/2 organic lemon

1–2 teaspoons strong mustard (Dijon!)

salt, freshly ground pepper

1 garlic clove

4–5 tablespoons olive oil

1 Wash the lemon under hot water and
grate the zest. Squeeze out the juice.
Combine both with the mustard and a little
salt and pepper.

2 Peel the garlic, push it through a garlic
press, and add. Slowly mix in the olive oil
and 1 tablespoon water, using a whisk.

Time you need: 10 minutes
Goes well with: grilled eggplant, zuccini,
white beans, squid...
Calories per portion: 95

Delicate variation on the lemon dressing:
Rinse and pat dry 3–4 anchovy filets. Finely
chop and mix in. Produces a fine, not a fishy
taste—delicious with white beans.

Egg dressing
Almost a small salad in itself

Enough for 4:

2 hardboiled eggs

3 tablespoons white wine vinegar

1 tablespoon mustard

1 tablespoon sour cream

salt, freshly ground pepper

5 tablespoons oil (sunflower oil, olive oil)

a few basil leaves

1 Shell the eggs and very finely dice.

2 Combine the vinegar, mustard, sour
cream, salt, and pepper. Slowly whisk in the
oil; add the eggs.

3 Wash the basil leaves, cut into thin strips,
and mix in.

Time you need: 10 minutes
Goes well with: warm asparagus, lamb's
lettuce, fresh mushroom slices, watercress
or as a sauce with cold cuts and ham
Calories per portion: 135

Potato salad
The one and only?

Hardly. But one of the most delicious of its kind.

Serves 4 very hungry people as the ultimate side dish:

2 pounds potatoes (waxy variety)

salt

1 cup meat stock

4 tablespoons white wine vinegar

1 teaspoon strong mustard

freshly ground pepper

1 onion, 1 bunch chives

3–4 tablespoons sunflower oil

1 Wash the potatoes, place in a saucepan, cover with water, add 1 teaspoon salt, cover, and bring to a boil. Cook covered over a medium heat for 15–20 minutes. Drain, leave to cool briefly, and peel while still quite hot.

2 Meanwhile heat the stock and season with vinegar, mustard, salt, and pepper. Peel and finely chop the onion. Wash and chop the chives.

3 Slice the warm potatoes—don't worry about them falling apart, they will do that later anyway. Immediately pour over the

warm stock. Leave to infuse for a moment. Then mix in the oil, onion, and chives. Season to taste with salt, pepper, or vinegar. Devine!

Time you need: 45 minutes
Goes well with: roast pork and fried filet of fish, grilled sausages, roast chicken, and, and, and...
Calories per portion: 260

Pasta salad
A favorite at parties — for children and adults alike

Serves 6–8 hungry buffet guests:

1/2 pound fusili

salt

1/2 pound cooked ham

1/3 pound Gouda cheese

1 bunch radishes

1/2 cucumber

1 bunch chives, 1 bunch dill

2–3 tablespoons mayonnaise

2–3 tablespoons yogurt

2–3 tablespoons white wine vinegar

freshly ground pepper

2–3 tablespoons sunflower oil

1 Pour the pasta into boiling salted water and cook uncovered according to the instructions on the package, until they are *al dente*. Drain in a colander, rinse with cold water, drain.

2 Meanwhile, remove the fat from the ham, cut into strips. Grate the cheese. Wash and trim the radishes, and slice. Peel the cucumber and finely dice. Wash and chop the herbs.

3 Combine the mayonnaise (home-made mayo is obviously the best—recipe on page 92), the yogurt, and the vinegar. Season to taste with salt and pepper. Whisk in the oil.

4 Mix the pasta with all the other ingredients, pour over the sauce, and leave to infuse (not too long, if the salad has been prepared with home-made mayonnaise!). Before serving, check if something needs to be added...salt, pepper, vinegar?

Time you need: 30 minutes
Goes well with: everything else on the buffet
Calories per portion: (8): 310

Bread salad from Tuscany
Culinary recycling

Serves 4–6 hungry folk as an appetizer:

5 slices stale Italian white bread

1 pound ripe tomatoes

1 small red, 1 small green bell pepper

1 bunch scallions

1 bunch parsley, 1 bunch basil

2 garlic cloves

2–3 tablespoons red wine vinegar

salt, freshly ground pepper

5 tablespoons good olive oil

1 tablespoon capers

1 Dice the stale bread. Wash, trim, and dice the tomatoes and bell peppers. Wash and trim the scallions; cut into fine strips. Mix everything.

2 Wash and finely chop the herbs. Peel and chop the garlic. Mix the vinegar with salt and pepper, whisk in the oil. Mix with the capers and the bread, chill.

Time you need: 30 minutes and about
1 hour chilling time or longer
Goes well with: a glass of red wine
Calories per portion (6): 150

Arabian bulgur salad
Refreshing & easy

Serves 4 hungry and curious people:

1 cup bulgur wheat

1 large bunch scallions

1 pound tomatoes

5–6 tablespoons lemon juice

salt, freshly ground pepper

about 1/2 teaspoon chili powder

1 big pinch cumin (completely different from

the usual caraway seeds—indispensable for

Indian dishes)

1 teaspoon dried green mint (or a few

chopped fresh mint leaves)

6 tablespoons good olive oil

1 bunch parsley

1 Pour the bulgur wheat into a bowl, cover with cold water, and leave to swell for about 1 hour, until the grains have become soft but are still firm to the bite.

2 Wash and trim the scallions. Finely chop. Wash and finely dice the tomatoes, removing the green stem ends.

3 Drain the bulgur wheat in a very fine strainer, stir vigorously with a spoon, and press for the water to drain. Mix the bulgur wheat with the scalions and the tomatoes.

4 Combine the lemon juice with salt, pepper, chili powder, cumin, and mint. Mix with the bulgur wheat, stir in the oil. Season to taste. Wash fresh parsley, coarsely chop or tear the leaves apart, and add. It tastes best chilled.

Time you need: 20 minutes plus
1 hour swelling time
Goes well with: broiled lamb, duck breast
Calories per portion: 330

Cucumber salad
The all-time summer favorite

Serves 4 hungry people as a side dish:

1 big cucumber

1 onion

3–4 tablespoons yogurt

2–3 tablespoons white wine vinegar

salt, freshly ground pepper

3 tablespoons sunflower oil

1 bunch dill

1 Peel and trim the cucumber. Slice or grate. Peel, halve, and thinly slice the onion.

2 In a salad bowl combine the yogurt with the vinegar, salt, and pepper. Whisk in the oil. Mix in the cucumber and onions. Leave to infuse for a moment.

Time you need: 10 minutes
Goes well with: meat, fish, other salads
Calories per portion: 95

Cabbage and red pepper salad
Lots of salad for very little money

Serves 6 hungry people as a side dish:

1 white cabbage (2 pounds), salt

2 red bell peppers

1 big bunch parsley

5–6 tablespoons white wine vinegar

salt, freshly ground pepper

5–6 tablespoons sunflower oil

1 Remove the outer leaves of the cabbage. Quarter and cut out the stalk. Slice the cabbage, using a vegetable grater. Place into a salad bowl, season with salt, and knead with your fingers to make the cabbage more tender without loosing its crispness.

2 Wash the red peppers and cut into thin strips. Wash and finely chop the parsley. Mix with the cabbage.

3 Mix the vinegar with the pepper, whisk in the oil. Pour over the salad, stir and leave to steep. Season to taste.

Time you need: 30 minutes
Goes well with: roast pork, hamburgers
Calories per portion: 115

String bean salad
Grandma's recipe

Serves 4 hungry people as an appetizer or side dish:

1 1/2 pounds tender string beans, salt

a few stems fresh savory

2 onions, 2 ounces bacon

3–4 tablespoons white wine vinegar or cider vinegar

freshly ground pepper

2–3 tablespoons sunflower oil

1 Wash the beans, trim the ends—if there is a string, remove it.

2 Bring to a boil 2 quarts water, add salt and the savory. Add the beans and cook covered for 10–12 minutes. Rinse under cold water. Peel and chop the onions; mix with the beans.

3 Finely dice the bacon and fry over a medium heat until crispy. Add the vinegar and pour over the salad. Season to taste with salt and pepper, mix in the oil.

Time you need: 30 minutes
Goes well with: fried potatoes, roast meat
Calories per portion: 190

Beef salad with pumpkin seed oil
Left-overs feast

Serves 4 as a snack:

1 pound left-overs of boiled beef (see page 80, noodle soup)

2 small onions

2 gherkins, 1 tablespoon capers

2–3 tablespoons white wine vinegar

2 tablespoons sunflower oil

2 tablespoons pumpkin seed oil

salt, freshly ground pepper

1 bunch chives

1 Cut cold boiled beef into thin strips. Peel the onions and cut into thin rings. Very finely chop the gherkins. Mix everything and add the capers.

2 Combine the vinegar, both oils, salt and pepper. Pour the dressing over the salad and leave to steep. Wash and chop the chives and sprinkle over the salad.

Time you need: 20 minutes
Goes well with: crusty bread
Calories per portion: 310

Variations:

Cucumber salad without oil
Bring to a boil 10 tablespoons apple, cider, or coconut vinegar adding 1 tablespoon sugar; leave to cool. Peel the cucumber, cut in half lengthwise. Remove the seeds with a spoon, slice the cucumber halves. Peel 2 red onions and cut into rings. Crumble 2–3 small dried chilies, mix with the vinegar, pour over the salad, and leave to infuse for a moment. Very refreshing, quite hot, ideal with rice dishes cooked in a wok!

Beans without bacon
Instead of the bacon use 1 can tuna in brine. Drain and mix in. Goes well with 1 pressed garlic clove in the dressing.
Or: Dress with the tomato vinaigrette (recipe on page 72).

Thai beef salad
Mix the strips of beef with lots of finely chopped scallions. For the dressing combine 4 tablespoons lemon juice, 2 tablespoons oil, 2–3 crumbled dried chilies, 2–3 chopped garlic cloves, and 1 pinch sugar. Sprinkle the salad with fresh cilantro leaves.

Pickled herrings
Nice breakfast after a party

Serves 4 hungry or hung-over people

6 fresh herrings

2 gherkins, 2 small onions

1 apple, 2 tablespoons lemon juice

2/3 cup sour cream, 1/2 cup yogurt

1 tablespoon horseradish (from a jar or freshly grated)

4 tablespoons white wine vinegar

3–4 tablespoons sunflower oil

salt, freshly ground pepper

1 bunch dill, chives, or parsley

1 Chop the herrings, slice the gherkins. Peel the onions and cut into thin rings. Wash the apple, quarter, and slice crosswise. Sprinkle with lemon juice.

2 Combine the sour cream, yogurt, horseradish, vinegar. and oil, slightly season with salt and pepper. Stir all the ingredients into the sauce, leave to infuse 1–24 hours. Wash and chop the herbs; sprinkle over the salad.

Time you need: 20 minutes + infusing time
Goes well with: bread, baked potatoes
Calories per portion: 480

Chinese fondue
A feast!

And a healthy one—because the ingredients of a "hot pot" are not dipped into oil, but into freshly prepared chicken stock. If you don't have the time, buy ready-made chicken stock and dilute 1:2 with water.

Serves 5 guests and 1 host:

1 ounce dried shiitake mushrooms (tongku)

2 ounces glass noodles

3/4 pound turkey breast filets

3/4 pound beef tenderloin

3/4 pound fish fillets (e. g. salmon, tuna, halibut)

1–2 jumbo shrimp for each person

2 bunches scallions

3/4 pound carrots

1 small Chinese cabbage

(or other fresh vegetable, such as spinach, kohlrabi, leeks)

about 3 quarts chicken stock (see Basic Tip)

Marinades, sauces, side dishes:

Soysauce, sesame oil, peanut oil, sherry or sake, grated fresh ginger, chopped garlic, lemon juice, freshly ground pepper, chili powder...

Asian ready-made sauces like plum sauce, sambal oelek...

fresh chilies

1 Soak the mushrooms in water, later remove the stalks. Briefly also soak the noodles, drain in a colander, and cut with kitchen scissors. Cut the meat and the fish into thin strips and place each kind in a separate bowl. Clean all the vegetables and cut into matchsticks.

2 Prepare some marinades for the meat and the fish. For the fish, mix 2 tablespoons each: soysauce, sesame oil, and lemon juice. Or for the beef: 2–3 chopped garlic cloves, chili powder, freshly ground pepper, and 2–3 tablespoons peanut oil. And for the chicken perhaps 2 tablespoons lemon juice, 2 tablespoons sesame oil, 1 tablespoon chopped fresh ginger.

3 In fact, you don't actually need any marinades—meat and fish taste delicious if you just dip them in the stock as they are, not least because a hot pot is accompanied by wonderful sauces.

4 But we haven't quite reached this point yet: First, the stock has to boil in a saucepan and be transferred to the fondue pot on the spirit burner. All the ingredients and sauces are by now in little bowls, the soysauce is on hand. Wash fresh chilies and cut into rings— some really do like it hot!

5 Every guest must have a little strainer on a stick—with a normal fondue fork you would simply be lost! Dip in the hot stock whatever takes your fancy and cook it for 1–2 minutes. Try everything! And at the end the climax: Everybody shares the rest of the hot stock—full of the lovely flavor of everything that was cooked in it.

Time you need: stock 2 hours 30 minutes (but does not need attention), active work 1 hour
Goes well with: rice
Calories per portion: 340

Basic Tip

Home-made chicken stock

In a large saucepan bring 4 quarts water to a boil. Add 2 peeled and halved onions, 2 bayleaves, 1 tablespoon salt, a few pepper corns. Place a boiling chicken (3 pounds) in the pan, cover and simmer over a low heat for about 1 1/2 hours. Wash and trim 2 bunches soup vegetables and dice. Add to the chicken, and simmer uncovered for another hour, skimming away the scum occasionally. Remove the chicken (tastes very nice cold and diced with lemon dressing, on page 73), and strain the broth using a fine strainer. Skim the fat with a spoon or blot with paper towels. Season to taste with salt, pepper and — a dash of lemon juice!

Noodle soup
Very comforting

Serves 4 hungry people:

1 pound beef bones, salt

1 1/2 pounds brisket

1 bunch herbs and vegetables

for making soup

2 onions

3 dried chilies (for those who like it hot)

peppercorns

1 bunch scallions

freshly ground pepper

6 ounces soup noodles

1 Rinse the bones and place them in a large saucepan, add 2 quarts cold water and salt, cover, and bring to a boil. Simmer over a very moderate heat for about 1 hour. Skim off the scum regularly.

2 Wash and roughly chop the soup vegetables. Peel and quarter the onions. Crumble the chilies. Add the vegetables, chilies, and some peppercorns to the meat and continue to simmer gently for another hour.

3 Wash and trim the scallions, then cut them into thin strips.

4 Remove the meat from the broth and cut into strips. Strain the broth to remove the excess fat swimming on top. Bring to a boil again, and season to taste with salt, pepper, and chilies.

5 Place the noodles in the boiling broth and cook for a few minutes, according to the instructions on the package. Add the meat and scallions and reheat for 1 minute.

Time you need: a good 2 hours, but only about 30 minutes of work
Goes well with: bread or rolls
Calories per portion: 350

Minestrone — a speedy version
Get ready, get your spoons...

Serves 4–6 vegetable fans:

1 1/2 quarts ready-made vegetable stock

1 pound potatoes, 1 young leek

2 medium carrots

2 small zucchini

2 celery sticks

2 ripe tomatoes

1 can (8 ounces approx.) beans (white or red)

salt, freshly ground pepper

2 teaspoons pesto

1/4 cup Parmesan or Pecorino cheese, freshly grated!

1 Pour the stock into a large saucepan, cover, and bring to the boil.

2 Wash, peel, and finely dice the potatoes; add to the stock. Cut the leek lengthwise, wash, cut in strips, and add. Peel and slice the carrots; add. Wash and trim the zucchini and celery, cut into strips or slice; add.

3 Immerse the tomatoes in a bowl of boiling water for 30 seconds, then cold water for 1 minute until cool enough to peel off the skins. Dice the tomatoes and place together with the drained beans in the soup, which has become thick and colorful. Cover and simmer over a gentle heat for another 15–20 minutes. Season to taste with salt and pepper. Stir in the pesto and the grated cheese at the very end.

Time you need: 45 minutes
Goes well with: good fresh bread
Calories per portion (6): 280

Potato soup
Very cheap, very nice

If you want to spend a little more, add 3/4 ounce dried porcini mushrooms. Soak, chop, and briefly cook. Exciting touch!

Serves 4 really hungry people:

1 1/3 pounds potatoes, 2 onions

1 leek, 2 carrots

1/4 pound bacon

1 tablespoons clarified butter

1 1/2 quarts meat stock

1 bayleaf, marjoram (dried 1/2 teaspoon, fresh a little more)

salt, freshly ground pepper

freshly grated nutmeg

1 Peel the potatoes and finely dice. Peel the onions and finely chop. Cut through the leek lengthwise, wash thoroughly, and cut into very thin slices. Peel the carrots and finely dice. Dice the bacon.

2 In a saucepan melt the clarified butter over a medium heat. Sauté the bacon and the onions. Stir in the vegetables, a small portion at a time, and cook briefly. Pour in the stock. Add the bayleaf, dried majoram, salt, and pepper. Cover and simmer for 30 minutes.

3 Lightly purée the soup when it is cooked. Season to taste with salt, pepper, and nutmeg—and if you have fresh marjoram, sprinkle it over the soup now.

Time you need: 1 hour
Goes well with: sausages and bread
Calories per portion: 340

Tomato soups
Can take 12 minutes or 12 hours

Serves 4 impatient soup fans:

1 onion, 2 tablespoons oil

1 large can peeled tomatoes (28 ounces approx.)

1 pint meat stock

1/4 pound Roquefort cheese

salt, freshly ground pepper

1/2 teaspoon sambal oelek

1 Peel and finely chop the onion. Sauté in hot oil. Add the tomatoes with their juice; chop in the pan. Add the stock and heat for 5 minutes. Dice the cheese and slowly stir in. Season to taste with salt, pepper, and sambal.

Serves 4 patient soup fans:

2 onions, 2 garlic cloves

2 pounds really ripe tomatoes

1 tablespoon chopped basil leaves

salt, freshly ground pepper

2 ounces cooked ham

4 tablespoons olives

2 teaspoons tomato paste

3 cups chicken stock

1 pinch sugar

2–3 tablespoons gin

4 tablespoons heavy cream

1 Peel and chop the onions and the garlic. Wash and roughly dice the tomatoes, mix with the onions, garlic, and basil. Season to taste with salt and pepper, cover; chill for 12 hours.

2 Dice the ham and fry in hot oil over a low heat. Stir in the tomato mixture and the tomato paste, pour in the stock. Gently simmer for 5 minutes. Season to taste with salt, pepper, and gin. Slightly beat the cream and stir in.

Time you need: 12 minutes or 12 hours
Goes well with both: garlic croûtons (fry diced white bread in hot butter with chopped garlic until crispy)
Calories per portion: for the impatient 180, for the patient 185

Fresh fish soup
Gets you going!

The vital part of a good soup is the stock, the broth—and you cannot beat a home-made one.

Makes 1 quart fish stock:

2 pounds fish trimmings (heads and bones of nice nonoily fish—not salmon; ask your fishmonger to remove the gills, because they would make the stock taste bitter)

1 onion

2 garlic cloves

1 leek

1–2 carrots

2 celery stalks

1 small fennel

1 pint dry white wine

2 bayleaves

1 teaspoon white peppercorns

salt

1 Thoroughly wash the fish trimmings and place in a large saucepan. Peel and chop the onion. Cut the leek lengthwise, wash, and slice. Peel and cut the carrots. Wash and trim the celery and fennel, and slice.

2 Add the vegetables, bayleaves and peppercorns to the fish, pour in 5 cups water and the wine. Cover and bring to the boil. When boiling, remove the lid and simmer for 20–30 minutes over a medium heat. Regularly skim off the scum. Strain, pour back into the pan, and continue to simmer until the stock is reduced to about 1 quart. Season to taste with salt.

How to turn the stock into a soup for 4:

1 onion

2 garlic cloves

2 carrots

1 small leek

2 celery stalks

2–3 tablespoons olive oil

salt, freshly ground pepper

1–2 tablespoons crème fraîche

1 pound filet of fish (whatever there is, this time salmon would be OK)

1 handful fresh chervil or arugula

1–2 tablespoons lemon juice

1 Peel and finely chop the onion and the garlic. Wash and trim the vegetables and cut into matchsticks. Place in a wide saucepan and sauté in hot olive oil. Pour in the stock, season to taste with salt and pepper, cover, and cook for 3–4 minutes. Reduce the heat and stir in the crème fraîche.

2 Cut fish into 3/4–1-inch pieces. Place in the stock and gently simmer over a low heat for 3–5 minutes. Clean, wash, and finely chop the chervil or arugula. Gently stir into the soup together with the lemon juice, making sure the fish is not disintegrating.

Time you need: for the stock 1–1 1/2 hours, for the soup 40 minutes
Goes well with: fresh white bread
Calories per portion: 310

Pumpkin soup
Very quick & very good

Serves 4 hungry people in the fall:

2 1/2 pounds pumpkin, the bright orange butternut squash is the most delicious

1 onion

2 tablespoons butter

1 quart vegetable stock

salt, freshly ground pepper

lemon juice or balsamic vinegar

Gazpacho
Tastes of sun and Andalusia

Serves 4 hungry people during a heat wave:

1 3/4 pounds really ripe tomatoes

1 cucumber

1 green bell pepper

2 onions

3 garlic cloves

3 slices white bread

1–2 tablespoons red wine vinegar

3 tablespoons olive oil

salt, freshly ground pepper

1 tablespoon butter

1 Peel and seed the pumpkin, remove the tough fiber in the center. Dice the rest.

2 Peel and finely chop the onion. Melt the butter in a large saucepan. Briefly sauté the onions, mix in the pumpkin. Pour in the stock, cover, and bring to a boil. Simmer over a medium heat for 10–15 minutes, until the pumpkin is soft.

3 Purée in the pan, using a hand-held blender. Season to taste with salt, pepper, lemon juice or balsamic vinegar.

Time you need: 30 minutes
Goes well with: for a change, season to taste with ginger, curry, soy sauce or sprinkle with toasted flaked almonds
Calories per portion: 130

Cream of asparagus soup
A real smoothie

Serves 4 hungry people to start their meal:

1 pound asparagus

salt, 1 pinch sugar

1 bunch scallions

1 tablespoon butter

1 level tablespoon flour

2 tablespoons crème fraîche or sour cream

freshly ground pepper

1 tablespoon lemon juice

1 tablespoons chopped chives

1 Wash, peel, and slice the asparagus. Bring to the boil 1 quart water, add salt and a pinch of sugar. Cook the asparagus covered, until soft (it will probably take around 20 minutes).

2 Meanwhile, wash, clean, and trim the scallions and slice into thin rings.

3 Drain the asparagus and purée. Reserve the cooking liquid. Melt the butter, add the flour to make a roux. Mix in the onion rings. Slowly pour in the cooking liquid, stirring constantly to avoid it going lumpy.

4 Simmer for 10 minutes. Now add the asparagus purée, the crème fraîche or sour cream, and season to taste with salt, pepper, and lemon juice. Sprinkle with chives.

Time you need: 45 minutes
Calories per portion: 80

1 Put 2–3 tomatoes aside for later. Immerse the other tomatoes in a bowl of boiling water for 30 seconds, then cold water for 1 minute until cool enough to peel off the skins. Dice the tomatoes.

2 Wash the cucumber and halve, put one half to the side. Peel the rest and dice. Wash, seed, and halve the bell pepper. Dice one half.

3 Peel and chop 1 onion, peel the garlic. Purée both in a blender together with the chopped vegetables. Sprinkle 2 slices of bread with the vinegar and 2/3 cup water. Add together with the oil and purée until smooth. Season to taste with salt and pepper, cover, and chill for 2–3 hours.

4 Very finely dice the rest of the vegetables. Dice the rest of the bread and fry in butter until crispy. Mix the vegetables and the bread with the cold soup.

Time you need: active working time 45 minutes, cooling time 2–3 hours
Calories per portion: 200

Sauce
& Dip

I will only have good sauce and lots of it...

S s

What about sauce?

"Not needed. Meat, fish, fried eggs—perfectly OK without one."

But a roast without sauce would only be half as interesting.

"But a lot less work. You go in the kitchen with an armload full of stuff, and four hours later you emerge with a cupful of sauce."

Do you like music?

"Yes—and?"

Well, just as it's possible to survive without music, you can also live without sauces. But for a lot of people they're what really make a dish.

"Get to the point."

Someone who knows how to combine the best ingredients to produce a good sauce is a real cooking artist.

"Chinese and Italians are still artists even without lots of sauce."

OK, then do your frying with soy sauce or pesto.

"H'mm, I think I would rather have some of yours. Lots in fact!"

I will only have good sauce and lots of it.

"Then next time I'll cook with lots of good sauce."

Oh, really.

Our favorite ingredient

The egg

Spanish huevo; French oeuf;
Italian uovo

Here's what it is
- in this book, only eggs from chickens
- it starts with the yolk, and then builds up 4 layers of egg white and the shell on its way through the chicken
- divided into six weight classes (USDA): Peewee (15 oz.), Small (18 oz.), Medium (21 oz.), Large (24 oz.), Extra Large (27 oz.), Jumbo (30 oz.)

Here's what it has
- 75 calories per 24 ounces egg
- 6.7 grams of valuable protein
- 5 grams of fat, 2 grams saturated fatty acids
- 213 milligrams cholesterol
- lots of calcium, phosphorus, iron, vitamins A, D, E, and B12, riboflavin, phosphorus

Here's what it does
- absorbs air when beaten, and so lightens sauces
- becomes firm when heated and so can give substance to a hollandaise sauce
- can bind together—for example liquid and fat in mayonnaise
- great for dips when hard-boiled

Here's what it demands
- a happy mom. In other words a free-range chicken. All others are intensively reared.
- to be freshly laid. Use within five weeks of purchase
- to be stored in the refrigerator and warmed up in the kitchen before being cooked
- to be cooked well: soft in 3–4 minutes, medium in 5–6 minutes, and hard in 10 minutes.

Here's what it goes with
- a little acid in its sauce—from wine, vinegar, or lemon
- herbs like dill, tarragon, or chervil
- fatty foods like bacon, cheese, and butter
- salt—but only at the end of cooking; otherwise scrambled eggs become limp and fried eggs blotchy

Milk makes the sauce

Cream
The fat in milk (around 30% in cream) makes sauces taste both finer and more intensive. Whipped cream is, in addition, light and airy. This is why some people only use whipped cream in their sauces. Over time, however, this becomes somewhat fatty and dull. We think it is better to pep up your sauce by adding fresh cream right at the end, or to rely on your cooking skills and not to use any cream at all.

Crème fraîche
Special bacteria can thicken cream and make it into the slightly acid crème fraîche or, similar, thick sour cream. They are so thick and creamy that they can not only round off a sauce, but also bind it. Here the rule also is less is more.

Yogurt
In warm sauces yogurt rarely appears in anything other than slow cooking, where it can give an individual touch during the long cooking time. It is especially favored in the Far East—for example in Indian lamb curry. Cold sauces and dips are freshened by yogurt with its acid and lightened with its 3–4% natural fat. Those who prefer something fattier and milder should use sour cream instead.

and ...
... mascarpone is not exclusively for Tiramisu. A good spoonful of it will, for example, make a gorgonzola sauce milder and more interesting if added right at the end. Farmer cheese can also give dips and sauces a little more interest. And a sabayon with buttermilk instead of wine is something quite extraordinary.

Here comes the roux...

Anything good always comes back into fashion. But what was actually good about a roux? For a long time it was synonymous with boring mush which slid off the spoon. Then butter and cream were suddenly "in" and the sauce appeared saved. At first it was only butter and cream with a little pseudo-sauce which flowed onto our plates, so that was not quite right either.

Since then, trendsetters have rediscovered roux. This is because it will often turn a good base into a better sauce, which a heavy hand with butter does not. Antonin Carême is supposed to have invented it—the world's first celebrity chef, and a pretty smart guy. You would have to be, to work out the secrets behind roux.

The first of these is heat. This makes the flour ferment, so that it becomes sticky enough to bind. To prevent it from burning or softening, at first it is only cooked with hot fat. At high heat flour can absorb lots of fat. This prevents it from becoming lumpy in liquids later on.

And now the basic instructions for a fine roux sauce:

1 Melt 2 tablespoons of butter. Stir in 2 tablespoons of flour, which will bubble at first, and then produce a smooth, light colored, thick mass. For darker sauces it can now brown a little.

2 Now pour a pint of lukewarm liquid over it, while stirring well with a whisk. Keep stirring to avoid burning and bring to a boil quickly over a high heat.

3 Then, while stirring less, let it simmer for 10 minutes. This allows the flour to dissolve perfectly. The Carême Sauce is done.

Yes, we will
A good sauce base • or: stock cubes • better: a supply of ice-cubes of homemade sauce • courage when spicing • limiting to a little goodness • chutney • vegetable sauces (for example from puréed peas) • spoons for spooning, bread for dunking, potatoes for mashing • ALWAYS: mixing the remains on the plate with sauce and licking the plate clean (only among friends)

No, we won't
Ready-made sauces • the sauce pot as a catch-all for bad wine • monotonous spicing • daily institutional sauces • ingredient mish-mash • old garlic in dips • prosecco and arugula sauces (wine and grass sauces) • great steaks drowned in sauce • forgetting spontaneous super sauce recipes • NEVER EVER: white wedding with spaghetti Napoli (not even among friends)

Five simple five-minute sauces

Quick pasta sauce
Fry chopped garlic with oregano, add some tomato purée. Add canned tomatoes, olives, and a few capers, and anchovies. Bring to a boil, then add broken-up canned tuna and chopped parsley.

Quick sauce for fried fish
Grate a piece of cucumber, sauté it in the fat you fried the fish in, add plenty of white wine, and add a heaped spoonful of crème fraîche. Reduce until thick, then season with dill, mustard and salt.

Quick steak sauce
Caramelize shredded onion in the frying oil with a generous pinch of sugar, then douse with balsamic vinegar and a little stock and cook until syrupy. Pepper heavily, stir in basil, and turn the fried steaks in the sauce.

Quick steamed vegetable sauce
Toast curry and (if available) fennel seeds in a dry skillet, add a can of chopped tomatoes and a pot of yogurt, leave to cook for 5 minutes and season with salt and a little sugar. Mix with the vegetables, or cook them in the sauce.

Quick dip
Finely chop fresh mushrooms, and then stir to make a thick dip with a little lemon juice, lots of chives and pepper and some sweet and sour cream.
Tastes great with boiled potatoes, toast, or deep-fried snacks.

Green sauce
With seven herbs — never fewer!

Serves 4–6:

1 bunch chives

1/2 bunch parsley

1 handfull chervil

2–3 sprigs borage

4 sorrel leaves

5 sprigs lemon balm

2 hard-boiled eggs

1 cup crème fraîche

3 1/2 cups sour milk (or buttermilk)

1/4 cup mayonnaise

1 teaspoon strong mustard

Worcestershire sauce

salt, freshly ground pepper

1 Wash the herbs and shake dry. Remove the hard stems. Finely chop the herbs with a large knife on a big chopping board. Do not use a blender, or the herbs will taste bitter.

2 Shell and finely dice the eggs. Combine with the herbs and the rest of the ingredients, season to taste, and leave to infuse for 1 hour.

Time you need: to be active for 30 minutes, to relax for 1 hour
Goes well with: boiled potatoes, peeled or in their skins, boiled beef, fish
Calories per portion: (6): 255

Guacamole
Tex-Mex for beginners

Serves 4–6:

2 ripe avocados (soft, but not mushy)

6–7 tablespoons lemon juice

1 onion

2 garlic cloves

1–2 fresh chilies

2 medium-sized tomatoes

2 tablespoons olive oil

salt, freshly ground pepper

1 generous pinch ground cilantro

1 bunch parsley

1 Cut the avocados lenthwise, twist and separate the halves. Remove the pit and peel. If the avocados are soft enough, mash with a fork, if not, purée with a hand-held blender. Mix in the lemon juice immediately to prevent the avocados from turning brown.

2 Peel and finely chop the onion and garlic. Cut the chilies lengthwise, remove the seeds and stem. Wash and finely chop.

3 Immerse the tomatoes in a bowl of boiling water for 30 seconds, then cold water for 1 minute, until cool enough to peel off the skins. Very finely dice the tomatoes. Mix with the avocado purée and combine with the olive oil. Season to taste with salt, pepper and ground cilantro. Wash and finely chop the parsley and mix in.

Time you need: 25 minutes
Goes well with: tortilla chips, steamed fish, grilled meat, fried potatoes, cold meat, bread
Calories per portion (6): 100

Salsa verde –
the Italian version
of green sauce:

2 hard-boiled eggs are needed here too—and a handful of herbs, flat parsley is best. And to give it a Mediterranean touch, you add 5–6 anchovies, 2 garlic cloves, 3–4 tablespoons capers, and at least 5 tablespoons olive oil. First purée the egg yolks, parsley, anchovies, garlic, oil, and capers in a blender. Season to taste with 1–2 tablespoons white wine vinegar, salt, and pepper. Finely chop the egg whites and mix in. Ideal for fried fish, shrimp, Mediterranean vegetables.

Pesto
Make loads and store it in the freezer!

Pesto purists use a pestle and mortar to crush everything by hand. But a blender will do. Even if it's not perfect—it's so much faster!

Serves 4:

1 big bunch basil

2 tablespoons pine nuts

3 garlic cloves

salt

1/2 cup olive oil

1/4 cup Parmesan or

Pecorino cheese, freshly grated!

1 Pick the basil leaves from their stems. If necessary wipe with paper towels, but do not wash them.

2 Lightly toast the pine nuts without oil— remove from the heat when they start to give off their aroma.

3 Peel and slice the garlic. Purée in a blender with the basil, pine nuts, and a pinch of salt—or crush with pestle and mortar.

4 Transfer to a bowl, and bit by bit mix in the olive oil and the grated cheese, until the mixture turns into a smooth cream. Season to taste with salt—that's all!

Time you need: 20 minutes
Goes well with: spaghetti or other thin pasta, minestrone or other vegetable soups, fish, meat, or can be used as a sandwich spread
Calories per portion: 240

Basic Tip

Winter pesto:

Basically prepared in the same way as the summer pesto — but this time use parsley, shallots, walnuts or almonds, Swiss or Appenzell cheese, and sunflower oil instead of olive oil.

Tzatziki
Keep on hand

Serves 4:

3 cups yogurt (real Greek sheep's milk yogurt is best)

1 firm cucumber

salt, 3 garlic cloves

1 tablespoon white wine vinegar

1–2 tablespoons olive oil

1 The yogurt should become a little firmer in consistency and must therefore drain for a while. Put a paper coffee filter in a strainer, spoon the yogurt into the filter, and leave for a while.

2 Peel and grate the cucumber, place in a bowl, add 1 teaspoon salt, and leave to stand for 10 minutes. Transfer to a colander, and squeeze out as much water as possible, using a spoon. Mix with the yogurt.

3 Peel the garlic and using a garlic press, add to the bowl. Mix in the vinegar and oil, and season to taste with salt. If you like, you can add freshly chopped mint.

Time you need: 30 minutes
Goes well with: sesame bread, lamb, vegetables, potatoes
Calories per portion: 270

Mango chutney
Hot, sweet, delicious

If you don't eat it all yourself, put it into little jars for lovely presents!

Enough for 4 barbecue parties (2 quarts):

3 ripe mangoes (about 2 1/2 pounds)

1 ripe pineapple (2 1/2 pounds)

1 red bell pepper, 2 fresh red chilies

2 ounces fresh ginger

1/4 cup raisins

3/4 cup sugar, 1 tablespoon salt

1/2 cup fruit vinegar, 2–3 onions

1–2 garlic cloves, 2 lemons

1 teaspoon mustard seeds

1 teaspoon allspice

1 Remove the pits from the mangoes, peel, and dice. Scrape off any remaining flesh from the pits. Remove the flesh from the pineapple and dice.

2 Halve the bell pepper and the chilies lengthwise, remove the stem, seeds, and membranes. Wash and cut into small pieces. Peel and slice the ginger. Coarsely chop the raisins.

3 Place all the ingredients you prepared in a large saucepan, mix with sugar, salt, and vinegar, cover, and leave to marinade for a few hours or, even better, overnight.

4 Now peel and finely chop the onions and garlic. Squeeze the lemon. Add everything, including the spices, to the pan and mix well with the fruit.

5 Cover, and bring to a boil over a medium heat. Reduce the heat, uncover, and gently simmer for 30 minutes, until the chutney has the right consistency. Stir regularly and make sure that it does not burn.

6 If you want to keep the chutney, sterilize some jars with twist-off lids, fill with the chutney, and close immediately.
If not: Let it cool down and tuck in!

Time you need: to be active for 1 hour plus overnight marinading
Goes well with: everything barbecued, poultry, pork, fish, rice
Calories in total: 1840

Applesauce with gherkins
Ideal for barbecues

Serves 4:

1 Granny Smith apple

1 tablespoon lemon juice

1 onion

1–2 gherkins

3/4 cup sour cream

2–3 tablespoons mayonnaise

2 tablespoons horseradish (from a jar)

salt, freshly ground pepper

chives or dill

1 Peel, quarter, and finely dice the apple, sprinkle with lemon juice. Peel and finely chop the onion. Finely dice the gherkins.

2 Combine the sour cream, mayonnaise, and horseradish. Season to taste with salt and pepper, mix in the apple, onion, and gherkins. Wash and finely chop the chives or dill and stir into the sauce.

Time you need: 10 minutes
Goes well with: grilled meat, hamburgers
Calories per portion: 150

Peanut sauce
Will keep

Serves 4:

2–3 tablespoons sunflower oil

2 tablespoons mild curry paste (ready-made)

1 can unsweetened coconut milk (14 ounces approx.)

1 cup crunchy peanut butter

2 tablespoons sugar

salt

3 tablespoons rice or apple vinegar

1 Heat the oil in a small saucepan over a medium heat, stir in the curry paste, and briefly fry. Add the coconut milk, mix well, and gently simmer for 1–2 minutes.

2 Stir in the peanut butter, and season with sugar, salt, and vinegar. Continue to simmer for another 5–10 minutes, until the sauce is thick and creamy. Season to taste.

Time you need: 15 minutes
Goes well with: chicken satay or other Asian meat dishes, vegetable and rice
Calories per portion: 320

Tuna dip
A new twist

Serves 4:

1 can tuna in brine (6 ounces)

2 garlic cloves

2 tablespoons capers

2 tablespoons lemon juice

1 dash white wine

2 tablespoons olive oil

2 tablespoons crème fraîche

salt, freshly ground pepper

1 Drain the tuna. Peel and halve the garlic. Purée both in a blender with the capers, lemon juice, wine, and oil.

2 Stir in the crème fraîche, season to taste with salt and pepper.

Time you need: 10 minutes
Goes well with: fresh white bread, grissini, raw vegetables, veal, hot baked potatoes
Calories per portion: 150

Mayo
—homemade!
Very impressive

The eggs really have to be absolutely fresh, because the egg yolks will be eaten raw! If you want to use less oil, you can simply add a little yogurt at the end—then you will have fewer calories, but still a deliciously thick cream.

Serves 4:

1 very fresh egg at room temperature (only the egg yolk is needed for this recipe!)

1 pinch salt

1 teaspoon mustard

1/2–1 tablespoons lemon juice

1/2 cup oil (sunflower oil, olive oil)

1 Separate the egg, place the egg yolk in a bowl (the Basic Tip below suggests what you can do with the egg white). Season with salt, combine with the mustard, and 1/2 tablespoon lemon juice.

2 Continue with a whisk or a hand-held bender: Start by adding just a few drops of oil, then pour in a little more, while whisking continuously. The oil you are adding must immediately blend with the egg mixture and not form a little puddle on top of it. If it does, adjust the amount of oil you are adding.

3 The egg mixture will slowly turn into a thick, creamy mayonnaise. When you have used up all the oil, keep whisking until the consistency is exactly right. Season to taste with salt, pepper, and a little more lemon juice.

Time you need: 15 minutes
Goes well with: from BLT sandwiches to artichokes—it depends on what you like
Calories per portion: 170

Variations:

Garlic mayonnaise
Add peeled and pressed garlic cloves to the egg yolk right at the beginning. How many? How ever many you like—2 would be fine. Goes well with fried fish or a vegetable platter.

Lemon mayonnaise
Halve 1 lemon, squeeze one half, and combine with the egg yolk as described in the recipe on the left. Pare and very finely dice the zest of the other half and mix with the mayonnaise at the very end. This goes perfectly with fish, and also with cold meat.

Herb mayonnaise
Mix in plenty of freshly chopped herbs at the end: e.g. parsley, chives, lemon balm, dill, chervil, or basil. This tastes very good in combination with garlic. Goes very well with grilled summer vegetables, baked mushrooms, and can also be used as a sandwich spread.

Remoulade sauce
Finely chop 1–2 gherkins, 1/2 onion, 1 anchovy, some parsley, chives or dill together with 1 tablespoon capers and mix with the mayonnaise. Season to taste with pepper and strong mustard. Goes well with roast beef, breaded filet of fish, and all the other dishes mentioned above.

Basic Tip

You can use the egg white for a meringue or a giant portion of scrambled eggs (just mix it in with the other eggs).

Vegetable sauce from Provence
Easy going

You can use this sauce to roast meat in—after you have fried the meat over a high heat to seal in the juices, just pour over the sauce together with a little extra stock

Serves 4:

1/2 pound ripe tomatoes

1/3 pound eggplant

1/3 pound zucchini

1 small red or yellow bell pepper

1/4 pound onions

2–3 garlic cloves

3–4 tablespoons olive oil

1 sprig fresh rosemary

1/2 cup heavy cream

salt, freshly ground pepper

1 tablespoon balsamic vinegar

possibly 5–10 tablespoons vegetable stock

1 Immerse the tomatoes in a bowl of boiling water for 30 seconds, then cold water for 1 minute, until cool enough to peel off the skins. Dice the tomatoes. Wash and dice the eggplant and zucchini, removing the stem ends. Halve the bell pepper, remove the seeds and the membranes. Wash and dice.

2 Wash and finely chop the onion and garlic. Heat 2 tablespoons olive oil in a heavy roasting pan. Briefly sauté the onions and garlic. Add the rest of the vegetables and the sprig of rosemary. Pour in the remaining oil and 1/4 cup water, season to taste with salt and pepper. Cover and cook over a gentle heat for about 40 minutes.

3 Pour in the heavy cream, stirring well. Bring to a boil again uncovered, remove from the heat, and discard the rosemary. Season to taste with salt, pepper, and balsamic vinegar. If you wish to, you can purée the vegetables and turn them into a smooth sauce. If you prefer it runnier, dilute it with stock.

Time you need: 1 hour 15 minutes
Goes well with: lamb, baked potatoes, roast pork or fried fish
Calories per portion: 195

Spanish mojo
Whether red or green— it's really hot

Serves 4 or more:

4 medium garlic cloves

2–3 fresh red (or green) chilies

2 teaspoons sweet paprika (not for the green mojo!)

1/2 teaspoon ground cumin

1/2 teaspoon dried oregano (for green mojo: 2 tablespoons freshly chopped parsley or 1 tablespoon fresh cilantro)

3 tablespoons wine vinegar

3 tablespoons olive oil

salt, freshly ground pepper

1 Peel and chop the garlic. Halve the chilies lengthwise, remove the stems and seeds. Wash and chop.

2 Purée the chilies and the garlic with all the other ingredients and spices in a blender.

3 Add a few tablespoons of water, if needed. Season to taste with salt and pepper.

Time you need: 15 minutes
Goes well with: baked potatoes, broiled

94

meat, vegetables—or simply a portion of rice mixed with 2–3 teaspoons mojo, topped with fresh parsley and roasted pine nuts
Calories per portion: 75

Variation:

Hot tomato sauce
Immerse 1 pound tomatoes in a bowl of boiling water for 30 seconds, then cold water for 1 minute, until cool enough to peel off the skins. Dice the tomatoes and mix in the mojo.

Carrot & ginger sauce
Very fruity, quite hot

Serves 4:

1 small onion

1 thumb-sized piece fresh ginger

1 pound carrots

2 tablespoons oil, 1 teaspoon curry powder

1 cup vegetable stock

1/4 teaspoon ground cumin, sugar

chili powder to taste

salt, freshly ground pepper

1 juicy orange (to be squeezed)

1 Peel and finely chop the onion and ginger. Peel the carrots and finely slice.

2 Heat the oil in a saucepan. Sauté the onion and ginger for 1–2 minutes over a medium heat, stirring occasionally. Stir in the carrots and the curry powder and cook for 2 minutes, while stirring. Pour in the stock. Season to taste with cumin, a pinch of salt and a little chili powder, salt, and pepper.

3 Cover and simmer for 20 minutes. Remove from the heat and purée, using a hand-held blender or a mouli (picture top left).

4 Pour in the orange juice, bring back to a boil, stirring vigorously. Season to taste with salt and pepper.

Time you need: 35 minutes
Goes well with: chicken breasts, filets of fish, or simply a plate of rice, sprinkled with lots of freshly chopped parsley
Calories per portion: 90

Barbecue sauce
Unusual ingredients, perfect taste

Serves 4:

1 slice chilled watermelon (about 1 pound with the rind, 3/4 pound without)

2 onions

4–6 tablespoons tomato ketchup

1 teaspoon honey

salt, cayenne pepper

1 Peel and seed the melon. Purée in a blender.

2 Peel and coarsely chop the onion and place in the blender. Add the ketchup and and the honey and purée. Season to taste with salt and cayenne pepper. Serve immediately or chill.

Time you need: 10 minutes
Goes well with: everything grilled
Calories per portion: 50

Fresh pea sauce
Interesting and tasty

Fresh means straight out of the freezer! Pea pods from the garden are rare these days—and fresh snow peas would not be used to make a sauce, but eaten as a very nice vegetable. You briefly stir-fry them in butter and sprinkle them with fresh herbs.

Serves 4:

1 small onion

1 tablespoon butter

3/4 pound frozen peas

1/2 cup dry white wine

2/3 cup heavy cream

salt, freshly ground pepper

1/2 bunch basil

lemon juice

1 Peel, halve, and very finely chop the onion. Melt the butter in a deep saucepan over a medium heat and sauté the onion, stirring regularly.

2 Open the package of peas, and place the frozen peas in the saucepan. Mix with the onion, pour in the wine and the heavy cream. Season to taste with salt and pepper, cover, and bring to a boil.

3 Clean the basil leaves and add a few. Cover and simmer for 5 minutes.

4 Remove the saucepan from the heat, add the rest of the basil, and purée in the saucepan, using a hand-held blender. Season to taste with salt, pepper, and a dash of lemon juice.

Time you need: 15 minutes
Goes well with: soft-boiled eggs (still warm), boiled beef, salmon, pork tenderloin
Calories per portion: 190

Mushroom sauce
Does not keep!

Serves 4:

1 1/4 pounds fresh mushrooms

3 tablespoons lemon juice

1 onion

1 bunch parsley

2 tablespoons butter

salt, freshly ground pepper

1 cup heavy cream

1 Wipe the mushrooms with paper towels or scrape them with a knife, but do not wash them. Thinly slice the mushrooms and sprinkle with 2 tablespoons lemon juice to prevent discoloring. Peel and finely chop the onion. Wash the parsley and shake dry; finely chop using a big knife.

2 Melt the butter in a large skillet. Briefly sauté the onion until it turns transparent. Add the mushrooms, a handful at a time, and sauté while stirring. Season with salt and pepper, stir in half of the parsley and the heavy cream.

3 Gently simmer over a low to medium heat for 10 minutes. Season to taste with salt and pepper and the rest of the lemon juice. Sprinkle with fresh parsley.

Time you need: 30 minutes
Goes well with: pasta, dumplings, fried veal and pork, steak
Calories per portion: 210

Curry cream
Goes with almost everything

Serves 4:

1 small onion

1 tablespoon butter

1 tablespoon curry paste (ready-made)

or 2 tablespoons curry powder

1/2 cup dry white wine

1/2 cup chicken stock

1 cup heavy cream

salt, freshly ground pepper

lemon juice to taste

1 Peel the onion and chop as finely as possible. Melt the butter in a wide saucepan or skillet. Sauté the onion over a low heat until it turns transparent.

2 Stir in the curry paste or powder and mix well with the onion. Pour in the wine, increase the heat, and briefly reduce. Pour in the stock and the heavy cream, leave uncovered, and reduce again until the sauce turns creamy. Stir from time to time to prevent burning.

3 After 10–15 minutes the consistency of the sauce will be nice and creamy. Season to taste with salt and pepper and perhaps a dash of lemon juice. That's it!

Time you need: 25 minutes
Goes well with: turkey escalopes, chicken breasts, steamed fish, rice, and vegetables, pasta
Calories per portion: 190

Variation:

Hot curry sauce
How hot this sauce is going to be obviously depends on the type of curry mix you use. For those who really like it hot: Sauté 1–2 crumbled chilies, some garlic, and chopped fresh ginger with the onion— you'll have a beautifully Asian aroma. Goes very well with rice dishes with meat or vegetarian ones.

Cheese sauce
Really Basic

You can use a roux as base and reduce the sauce in calories! Recipe on page 87.

Serves 4:

1/2 pound Gorgonzola or Roquefort cheese

2/3 cup milk

salt, freshly ground pepper

2 tablespoons pine nuts

1 Dice the cheese and place with the milk in a saucepan. Melt over a very gentle heat, stirring frequently until the sauce turns creamy. Season with salt and pepper— and that's already it.

2 To improve, toast pine nuts in a skillet without fat and sprinkle over the sauce.

Time you need: 10 minutes
Goes well with: pasta, boiled potatoes, vegetables like leek, carrots, cauliflower
Calories per portion: 225

Hollandaise sauce
Really quite impressive

This light butter sauce is very versatile—
you can add whatever you like: e.g. capers,
a dash of white wine, a spoonful of mustard
or fresh herbs.

Serves 4:

2 sticks butter

3 egg yolks

salt, freshly ground pepper

2–3 tablespoons lemon juice

1 Start with the bain-marie: Fill a large
saucepan half with water and bring just to
a boiling point (when tiny little bubbles start
rising), but do not boil vigorously. Get a
metal bowl ready that fits in the saucepan.

2 In another saucepan, slowly melt the
butter, while constantly skimming off the
white froth on top.

3 Place the egg yolks in the metal bowl and
whisk with 1 tablespoon water. Transfer the
bowl to the hot water of the bain-marie.
Now add the melted butter, very little at
a time, stirring vigorously either with a hand-
held blender or an electric mixer. When it
looks like a foamy sauce, the deed is done—
you now only need to season with salt,
pepper, and lemon juice. Very nice!

Time you need: 20 minutes
Goes well with: all sorts of vegetables—
it is the classic sauce for cooked asparagus,
nice with steaks and steamed fish
Calories per portion: 430

Basic brown sauce
Always have some
in reserve!

It forms the base of lovely sauces for meat, poultry and pasta—improve with heavy cream, red wine, port, or cognac, season with mustard, onions, bacon, mushrooms, or paprika.

Makes 1 quart dark stock:

3 tablespoons oil

1 pound veal bones (chopped into smaller
pieces by the butcher)

1 small leek

3 carrots

1 celeriac (1/2 pound)

2–3 onions

2 tablespoons tomato purée

1–2 bay leaves

1 teaspoon peppercorns

1 bunch parsley

1 teaspoon salt

1 Use a big heavy saucepan (a Dutch oven is fine) and place it on the largest burner. Pour in the oil and heat. Add the bones and fry over a high heat on all sides, for at least 10–15 minutes, while stirring.

2 Meanwhile, prepare all the vegetables: Cut the leek lengthwise, wash thoroughly, and trim. Peel the carrots, peel the celeriac and wash. Coarsely chop. Peel and quarter the onions.

3 Add the vegetables to the bones and fry together for 5 minutes. Then pour off the oil and put the saucepan back on the heat. Stir in the tomato purée, bay leaves, and peppercorns. Cover with water and reduce uncovered over a medium heat.

4 When the water has almost boiled away, pour in more and let it boil away again. The more often you do this, the darker and richer the stock becomes.

5 After 1 hour wash the parsley and add. Simmer for another hour or so, continuously replacing the water.

6 Get a large strainer in a saucepan ready and strain the stock, reserving the broth. Reheat the stock and season to taste with salt. Remove the fat swimming on the top, using either a skimmer or some paper towels.

Time you need: 2 1/2 hours

Basic white sauce
Very handy to have

Improve with heavy cream or white wine, season with mustard, shallots, curry, or pesto—for pasta, poultry, vegetables.

Makes 1 quart white stock:

1 pound veal bones (chopped into smaller
pieces by the butcher)

1 small leek, 3 carrots

1 celeriac (1/2 pound)

2–3 onions

1–2 bay leaves

1 teaspoon peppercorns

1 bunch parsley

1 teaspoon salt

1 You need exactly the same ingredients for the white sauce as for the brown sauce— the difference is that you do not fry the ingredients at the beginning, but place everything immediately in water and simmer.

2 So put the bones and the cleaned and coarsely chopped vegetables in a large saucepan. Add the bay leaves, peppercorns, and washed parsley, cover with water, and bring to a boil. Simmer uncovered, regularly replacing the water.

3 After about 2 hours put everything through a strainer, reserving the broth. Briefly bring back to a boil, and season with salt. Remove the fat swimming on the top, either using a skimmer or some paper towels.

Time you need: 2 1/2 hours

Basic Tip
Both sauces keep for about a week in the fridge. To always have some in reserve, you can divide them into small portions and freeze.

Fish

Fish is more than just fish sticks

Here you will find anything that swims: in sea water (like codfish), in fresh water (like trout), or in both (like wild salmon); in the sea, in lakes, in ponds, in rivers, in streams; sometimes even in tanks in stores or restaurants!

But this is not the domain of Basic cooks. Looking for ready-to-cook fish, they prefer to check out the refrigerated counters or freezer lockers.

Which are fine, if they are not always coated with breadcrumbs and rectangular in shape.

Fish is more than just fish sticks. And it's more than just smoked salmon or tuna in brine.

Sometimes the best things that swim are not even fish. Crabs, mussels, squid: You will find them all here.

Only oysters, lobster, and caviar have been left out.

One can't have everything...

Five favorites

A quick guide for those of you who find yourselves lost at the fish counter

Flounder
- flat fish that live on the bottom of the ocean
- versatile: can be baked, broiled, pan-fried, deep-fried, or poached. The secret is not to overcook this fish

Salmon
- in the wild migrates from sea to river, today is mostly bred in fish farms. In the wild its color comes from eating large quantities of shellfish
- due to its high fat content it is ideal for frying and broiling (as a steak), but can also be poached

Red snapper
- high demand has led to high prices (and to fraudulent practices)
- excellent sweet, nutty flavor and firm texture—just make sure it really is red snapper

Codfish
- any dish that is just identified as "fish" is probably codfish: It is quite likely the most popular fish worldwide
- often underrated. It is especially good fried, but is also great poached or steamed
- tartar sauce and codfish are a perfect match

Tilapia
- fastest-growing aquaculture product in the U.S.A.
- readily available, this is another highly versatile fish that can be prepared using virtually any cooking method

Our favorite fish
The filet
Spanish filete; French
filet; Italian filetto

Here's what it is
• rarely a real filet, normally only a part of it; for the 6ft long codfish, only a tiny part
• around 3–5 ounces (without skin and bones) per filet

Here's what it has
• from a lean 78 calories (codfish) through to a moderate 100 (halibut) to a fat 217 (Atlantic salmon)
• lots of valuable protein
• usually almost no fat, sometimes lots of fat (eel, herring, mackerel, salmon), but always good fat
• plenty of vitamins A, D, E, and B, fluorine, iodine, and phosphorus

Here's what it wants
• to be really fresh
• to be stored as cold and for as short a time as possible
• to be cooked quickly and gently
• not to fight with other aromas

Here's what it likes
• butter, olive oil, cream—in moderation

• dill, tarragon, chervil, parsley, chives are great; bay leaf, oregano, rosemary, sage for rustic Mediterranean fish
• salt, a little pepper; curry, ginger, caraway, fennel seeds, paprika when appropriate
• mustard, soy sauce, other Asian sauces, Worcestershire sauce, sometimes pesto; wine, including red; vinegar and lemon (but not all the time)
• capers, anchovies, garlic, horseradish
• fennel, cucumber, leeks, bell peppers, mushrooms, spinach, tomatoes, zucchini, also in salads
• rice and potatoes, sometimes pasta
• preferably not: chili peppers, cheese, ketchup, sweet foods

Yes, we will
Try fish which doesn't taste fishy
• venture into the unknown: eating strange fish • fresh aspirations: eat sushi • do it ourselves: pickled, marinated, and soused fish • try tuna fish steak medium rare
• try grilled calamari • fish 'n' chips
• stockfish • fish filets with mustard sauce, fried fish with capers, lemon, garlic

No, we won't
Smelly fish disguised with lemon • restrict children to frozen fish sticks • serve finger-thick fish carpaccio • tuna from drag nets which trap dolphins • baked frozen calamari rings • eat mercury-containing fish more than once a month

How about a whole fish?

About 6 ounces fish per portion—this is true for filets. If you buy a whole fish, the rule is somewhat different. The advantages: It may well be fresher than a filet, because it is harder to disguise. The trimmings provide a good base for stock, sauce, or gravy. The disadvantages: lots of work if you have to filet it yourself. And you will be wasting money if you don't use the trimmings. Five calculations from worthwhile to waste:

58 percent yield from a 5 1/2 pound salmon: 8 ounces waste, 2 pounds trimmings for stock
leaves 3 pounds filet, for 7–8 portions

45 percent yield from a 2 pound walleye pike 4 ounces waste, 3/4 pound trimmings
leaves 1 pound filet, for 2–3 portions

40 percent yield from a 1 pound flounder 3/4 ounce waste, 1/2 pound trimmings (ideal for stock)
leaves 7 ounces filet, for 1–2 portions

14 percent yield from a 2 pound carp 4 ounces waste (too fatty), 1 pound trimmings
leaves 12 ounces filet, for 2 portions

Sushi
Handiwork for best friends

For practice: a rice snack rolled by hand or else shaped with a mat. It is best to use a bamboo mat from an Asian supermarket but if you need to you can use a dish towel or a paper napkin.

Makes 8 nigiri sushi and 16 maki sushi:

1 1/4 cups sushi rice (preferably Japanese round-grain rice; otherwise Italian risotto rice)

3 tablespoons light rice vinegar

sugar, salt

4 teaspoons wasabi powder (really hot, pale green Japanese horseradish, and found in Asian supermarkets!) or wasabi paste from a tube

For the 8 nigiri sushi with raw fish:

5 ounces superfresh tuna steak (or a salmon steak just as fresh, or ask at the fish counter)

For the 16 maki sushi with vegetables:

1/2 medium cucumber

2 medium carrots

3 tablespoons rice wine (sake) or rice vinegar

2 nori leaves (dried seaweed)

To garnish and as accompaniments:

chives, scallion pieces, avocado wedges, preserved ginger, soy sauce

1 Wash the rice in a strainer under cold water until the water runs clear. Leave to drain and dry in the strainer for 30 minutes. Then place in a saucepan, add 1 1/4 cups water and bring to a boil with the lid on. Allow to boil briefly and then reduce the heat, cover, and leave the rice to swell over a very low heat for 20 minutes. Add a little water if necessary.

2 Remove the rice from the stove, stir through with a wooden spoon, place in a bowl, and leave to cool thoroughly, or else spread the rice out on a cookie sheet so that it cools more quickly.

3 Combine the rice vinegar with 1 tablespoon sugar and 1 teaspoon salt in a saucepan, quickly bring to a boil and then remove from the stove immediately. Leave to cool and then drizzle over the cooled rice; mix in with a wooden spoon.

4 Mix the wasabi powder into a paste with 8 teaspoons water and leave to infuse.

5 Nigiri sushi: If using salmon (not necessary for tuna), feel for fish bones using your fingertips and remove any offenders with tweezers. Trim the edges of the fish. Then slice against the grain into 8 equal slices (any leftover strips can be used for the maki sushi). Thinly spread one side of each slice with the wasabi paste.

6 Shape about a half of the rice for the nigiri: Using a tablespoon divide the rice into 8 small portions (approximately bite-size), hold your hands under cold water for a short while and shape the rice portions into balls. Now take one piece of fish with the wasabi side upwards, place the rice ball on it, and

press. Turn it over and press down on the fish. Place on a platter.

7 Maki sushi: Peel the cucumber and carrot, slice the cucumber in half lengthwise and remove the seeds using a spoon. Slice both vegetables into slices about 2 inches long and 1/4 inch thick.

8 Bring the rice wine to a boil in a saucepan together with 2 tablespoons water, 1/2 teaspoon sugar, and 1/4 teaspoon salt. Simmer the carrot strips for 1 minute, then remove from the stove and add the cucumber pieces to the warm liquid. Leave to cool in the liquid.

9 Heat a nonstick skillet without any fat in it. Quickly brown the nori leaves on one side (not necessary if the leaves are preroasted, i.e. if they are described as "roasted" on the package). As soon as they begin to give off an aroma, remove them from the skillet and leave to cool. Then cut the leaves down the middle using kitchen shears.

10 Place one of the halved leaves shiny side down on a bamboo rolling mat so that the front edge is flush with the mat. Spread a very (watch out, it is very, very hot!) thin layer of wasabi paste over the leaf. Spread a portion of rice on top about 1/4 inch thick; leave a 1/2 inch wide margin on both sides lengthwise. Make a groove lengthwise in the upper third and place the vegetable strips or leftover fish strips in it.

11 Lift the bamboo mat and roll up the filled leaves one by one. Press down on the mat when removing them; cut the rolls in half with a sharp knife. Place the halves parallel next to each other and then halve both rolls again—the makis will then be the same size. Place cut side upward on the serving platter with the nigiris.

12 Garnish with chives, scallions, and avocado. Combine the remaining wasabi paste with the soy sauce and serve in small bowls for dipping. Serve with pickled ginger.

Time you need: 2 hours
Goes well with: green tea
Calories per sushi: nigiri: 100, maki: 35

Marinated salmon
Simply luxurious

Serves 7 guests and 1 host as an appetizer:

1 teaspoon white peppercorns

4 tablespoons kosher salt

3 tablespoons sugar

2 fresh salmon pieces with the skin (about
2 pounds in total weight—preferably a piece
from the middle because then they are the
same thickness throughout)

2 bunches dill

1 First of all find a suitable dish for the fish,
e.g. a baking dish or a flat bowl. Crush the
peppercorns with a pestle and mortar or else
grind them as roughly as possible with a
peppermill. Combine with the kosher salt
and the sugar.

2 Examine both salmon pieces with your
fingertips and remove any bones with
tweezers. Sprinkle the fish with the salt–
sugar–pepper mixture on both sides. Then
place one of the pieces of fish, skin
side down, in the dish.

3 Rinse the dill, shake dry thoroughly, and
chop finely. Sprinkle 2/3 of the dill over the

salmon in the dish and then place the second
piece of salmon skin side up on top. Sprinkle
with the remaining dill.

4 Cover the salmon in the dish with
aluminum foil, then weight it down securely.
Place in the fridge and leave to marinate for
2 days. Turn the salmon in the dish once or
twice a day, so that both fish pieces have
a turn to be at the bottom and become well
marinated.

5 And that's it! The slicing and serving are
actually more difficult than the preparation.
If you have a proper salmon knife then it's
a breeze: The long, narrow, flexible blade is
perfect for achieving superthin slices. But of
course you can do it with another, preferably
long sharp knife.

6 Remove the salmon from the marinade
and leave to drain. Place on a board with the
skin side down. With a long knife almost
level to the fish, slice the fish by drawing the
knife lengthwise along the salmon so that
you can turn out really thin salmon slices.

Time you need: 15 minutes active, 2 days
in the fridge, slicing depends on practice!
Goes well with: lemon quarters, creamed
horseradish, mustard sauce (mix coarse-
grain mustard with a pinch of sugar, white
wine vinegar, or lemon juice and oil and dill),
bread, crispy roast potatoes or pancakes
Calories per portion: 260

Shrimp cocktail
Foolproof

Serves 4 festive folk as an appetizer:

8 nice, crispy, fresh lettuce leaves

2/3 cup yogurt

4 tablespoons sour cream

2–3 tablespoons lemon juice

salt, freshly ground pepper

1 bunch dill or chives

3/4 pound cooked shrimp (peeled)

1 Wash the lettuce leaves and shake dry
thoroughly. Place 2 leaves in each goblet
or small bowl.

2 Combine the yogurt with the sour cream
and lemon juice, season lightly with salt and
pepper. Wash the dill or chives and shake dry,
then chop finely, and stir one-half into the
yogurt sauce.

3 Briefly rinse the shrimp and leave to drain
well in a colander. Then distribute them as
evenly as possible on the lettuce leaves,
pour the sauce over, and sprinkle with the
rest of the herbs.

Time you need: 15 minutes
Goes well with: crisp French bread
Calories per portion: 115

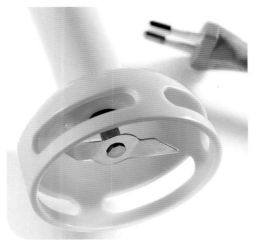

Fish balls
For the tapas platter

Serves 4 hungry people as an appetizer:

2 slices white bread, crusts removed
(one day old)

3/4 pound fish filets (e.g. codfish,
flounder, carp)

1/2 bunch parsley

2 tablespoons lemon juice

1 egg

salt, freshly ground pepper

1/2 teaspoon cilantro powder

1 tablespoon grated zest of an organic lemon

3 cups oil for frying

plus possibly some breadcrumbs

1 Break the white bread into small pieces and soak in cold water. Examine the fish with your fingertips and remove any bones with tweezers. Finely chop the fish.

2 Wash the parsley, shake dry, and chop finely. Squeeze the bread dry and purée together with the fish and the lemon juice in the mixer or with a hand blender. Stir the egg evenly into the mixture and then add the parsley. Season with salt, pepper, cilantro powder, and lemon zest.

3 Heat the oil in a saucepan, wok, or deep fryer. To test the temperature, place the handle of a wooden spoon in the oil: When small bubbles rise from the handle, the oil is hot enough for frying.

4 Shape the fish mixture into small balls (cool your hands under cold running water and roll a spoonful of fish purée between your hands). Place in the hot oil and wait to see what happens: If the ball falls apart, then the mixture is too soft and you need to add some breadcrumbs to make it more stable.

5 Now shape the rest of the mixture into small balls and fry them 4 or 5 at a time. Remove them after 3–4 minutes using a slotted spoon and immediately place them on a thick layer of paper towels. Serve hot, warm, or cold.

Time you need: 40 minutes
Goes well with: mojo, aioli, curry cream (pages 94, 96, 136), spicy preserved banana peppers, white bread...
Calories per portion: 360

Salted herring tartare
Quick & easy

Serves 4 hungry people as a quick appetizer:

6 single or 3 double salted herring filets
("matjes")

1 green or red bell peppers

1–2 red onions (or 1/2 bunch scallions)

4 tablespoons lemon juice

salt, freshly ground pepper

1 Slice the salted herring filets into tiny pieces using a large, sharp knife. Halve the bell peppers, removing the white membranes. Wash the pepper halves to remove the seeds. Slice the peppers into small pieces the same size as the fish pieces.

2 Peel the onions, cut in half and slice thinly, then chop finely. (Or clean the scallions and chop very finely.) Combine all of the ingredients and season lightly with a little salt and a lot of freshly ground pepper (even better: grind the peppercorns with a pestle and mortar.)

Time you need: 10 minutes (is even spicier if left to marinade for a while)
Goes well with: pumpernickel bread, beer
Calories per portion: 290

The quickest salmon in the world
Really Basic

Serves 4 hungry and very hurried people:

1 1/2 pounds salmon in a piece

5 tablespoons olive oil

salt, freshly ground pepper

1 lemon

1 Preheat the oven until really hot to 480 °F (or convection oven to 425 °F).

2 Slice the salmon into thin slices about 1/3 inch thick. Brush a cookie sheet with 2 tablespoons olive oil and lay the salmon slices on it next to each other, not on top of one another, or it won't work.

3 Season with salt, pepper, lemon juice, and drizzle the rest of the olive oil over the slices.

4 Place in the really hot oven (in the center) and roast for 2–3 minutes. That's it!

Time you need: 12–13 minutes
Goes well with: white bread or potatoes and salad, a light, dry white wine
Calories per portion: 495

Baked pepper fish
This one's easy too

Serves 8 hungry people:

4 garlic cloves, 1 1/2 lemons

8 fish filet slices (each 5–7 ounces, e.g. tilapia, codfish, flounder)

salt, freshly ground pepper

1 1/2 sticks soft butter, 3 tablespoons brandy

3 teaspoons preserved green peppercorns

4 tablespoons olive oil

8 tablespoons breadcrumbs

1 Peel and crush the garlic; squeeze the lemon. Season the fish with salt, garlic, and lemon juice.

2 Preheat the oven to 400 °F (also now: convection oven 350 °F). Combine the butter with the brandy and peppercorns; season.

3 Brush a cookie sheet with the olive oil and then place in the hot oven to heat up. Remove (using oven gloves!) and place the fish slices on it. Return to the oven (in the center) and bake for about 5 minutes.

4 Take the cookie sheet out and turn the fish over. Sprinkle with the breadcrumbs and dot with the pepper butter. Bake for a further 6–8 minutes. Serve with lemon wedges.

Time you need: 30 minutes
Goes well with: salad, white bread
Calories per portion: 560

Fish filets with lemon caper butter
For lemon fanatics

Serves 4 hungry people:

1 3/4 pound fish filets (e.g. flounder, codfish, tilapia)

salt, freshly ground pepper, sugar

1/2 bunch parsley, 1 organic lemon

1–2 tablespoons ghee, 3 tablespoons flour

3–4 tablespoons hard butter

1 tablespoon capers

1 Season the fish filets with salt and pepper. Wash the parsley and chop very finely. Wash the lemon under hot water, dry, grate the zest, and then squeeze.

2 Melt the ghee in a large nonstick skillet. Place the flour on a plate, flour the fish on both sides, shaking the pieces so that they are not coated in too much flour.

3 Place the fish in the hot ghee and fry over a high heat for about 1 minute. Then reduce the heat, carefully turn the filets over and fry for a further 2–4 minutes until they are opaque inside. Remove from the skillet, cover and keep warm.

4 Tip the crumbs from the frying out of the skillet and wipe it out with a paper towel. Place the lemon juice in the skillet and then add the cold butter in small portions with a spoon. Stir in the lemon zest, capers, and parsley. Season to taste with salt, pepper, and a pinch of sugar if necessary and then return the fish filets to the skillet briefly to warm them.

Time you need: 30 minutes
Goes well with: boiled potatoes
Calories per portion: 265

Flounder filets in saffron cream
Makes an impression

Serves 4 connoisseurs:

1 1/2 pounds flounder filets (more delicate but more expensive: sole filets)

3–4 tablespoons lemon juice

salt, freshly ground pepper

2 shallots, 1 tablespoon butter

3/4 cup fish stock (bought or make it yourself—see page 82) or a mixture of white wine and stock

1 cup heavy cream, 1 large pinch saffron

1 Drizzle the fish with 2 tablespoons lemon juice, season lightly with salt and pepper. Peel the shallots and chop very finely. Now place a large skillet on the stove (it will also need a lid to fit), melt the butter over a medium heat. Add the shallots and sauté until they are transparent.

2 Pour the fish stock into a skillet. Bring to a boil and then reduce the heat so that the liquid is just simmering.

3 Place half of the filets in the skillet, cover, and simmer for 2–3 minutes. Remove carefully, place on a platter, and cover. Simmer the remaining filets and keep warm. Quickly stir the heavy cream into the cooking liquid, add the saffron to 2–3 tablespoons of water and then to the cooking liquid. Simmer for 2 minutes until the sauce is light and creamy. Season with salt, pepper, and the remaining lemon juice and serve hot with the fish.

Time you need: 30 minutes
Goes well with: rice, arugula salad
Calories per portion: 400

Basic Tip

Classic cafeteria food, but really delicious:

Baked filet of ocean perch

Pat dry 4 ocean perch filets (just under 7 ounces each) with paper towels. Drizzle with lemon juice (2 tablespoons), season with salt and pepper. Dip the filets in flour (3 tablespoons) and shake off any surplus. Now dip into beaten eggs (2 medium-sized ones) on both sides, and finally coat in breadcrumbs. Lightly pat the coating to make it stick. Heat ghee (5-6 tablespoons) in a large skillet and fry the filets for 3-4 minutes on each side over a medium heat until golden brown. Serve with lemon wedges and potato salad (p74).

Whole fish in a salt coat

An invitation to a cooking event—admission:

1 pound of salt!

Coarse sea salt is usually recommended for this clever, age-old cooking method, but that very quickly makes the wrapping more expensive than the contents; a very acceptable substitute is kosher salt—actually the preferred choice of American professional chefs. The recipe is only worth attempting if you have a really good, fresh fish. The reward is that the original flavor is perfectly maintained.

Our tip: Plan to serve the lemon tart on page 161 for dessert. You will need two egg yolks for the tart and these are left over here—and anyway the tart is incredibly delicious after the fish.

Serves 4 hungry people:

1 nice large fresh, salmon trout or 2 smaller

ones (about about 2 1/2 pounds in total,

or use sea bass or sea bream)

1 bunch mixed fresh herbs

(e.g. parsley, basil, dill)

5 pounds salt

2 egg whites

3/4 stick butter

1–2 lemons

freshly ground pepper

1 Have the fresh salmon trout gutted when you buy it. When you get home, wash it again under cold running water and wipe dry with paper towels.

2 Quickly rinse the herbs. Place them in the fish's belly and then close the sides of the belly over one another so that the fish later lies on the bed of salt on its skin side only.

3 Preheat the oven to 480 °F (later: convection oven 430 °F).

4 And now the fun and games begin: Take out a large bowl and place all of the salt in it. Add the 2 egg whites and about 3/4 cup cold water and mix everything together well.

5 Fill an ovenproof dish the right size for the fish (or even a roasting pan) with the salt mixture to a depth of about 3/4 inch. Place the fish in the middle and coat completely with the rest of the salt dough, pressing it together well to enclose the fish.

6 Place in the hot oven (center) and leave there for about 30 minutes. Then turn the oven off, wedge the oven door with a cooking spoon so that it is open just a chink. Leave the fish to stand in its salt coat for another 10 minutes.

7 Melt the butter in a small saucepan. Cut the lemons into quarters and place on the table.

8 And now comes the best part—carefully break open the hard salt crust and free the supertender and supertasty fish from its salt shell. The salt-encrusted skin stays behind with the salt crust. The inside of the fish is unbelievably moist and tasty—place a portion for each person on a warm plate. Everybody helps themselves to the melted butter, fresh lemon juice, and a sprinkle of freshly ground pepper.

Time you need: 1 hour
Goes well with: potatoes, lettuce salad, a dry white wine—and the lemon tart
Calories per portion: 465

Thai trout baked in foil
Low in fat

Serves 4 hungry people:

4 trout (about 1/2 pound each), salt

3 carrots

1 piece fresh ginger

4 garlic cloves, 2 celery sticks

4 scallions

4 tablespoons oil

2 limes

1/4 teaspoon chili powder

2 tablespoons sake

4 tablespoons sweet soy sauce

1 Wash the trout under cold running water, drain them on paper towels. Rub with a little salt inside and out.

2 Peel the carrots, ginger, and garlic. Very finely chop the ginger and garlic. Wash and trim the celery and scallions. Cut the carrots, celery, and scallions into matchsticks

3 Preheat the oven to 400 °F (convection oven 350 °F). Place 4 large pieces of foil on the work surface, shiny side up. Brush with 1–2 tablespoons oil.

4 Squeeze 1 lime. Heat the rest of the oil in a small saucepan, stir in the chili powder, and fry for a few seconds. Pour in the sake, lime juice, and soy sauce, combine well, and remove from the heat.

5 Place each trout on a piece of foil. Sprinkle with the sauce inside and out. Put some of the vegetable sticks, garlic, and ginger inside the trout, and the rest on and around the fish.

6 Fold the foil and form sealed packages. Perforate the foil at the top with a small skewer or a fork so the steam can escape while cooking. Place in the center of the oven for 30 minutes.

7 Remove the trout packages from the oven and carefully open the foil, making sure that the juice does not run out. Transfer onto plates, sprinkle with the juice. Cut the second lime into 8 wedges and serve with the trout.

Time you need: 1 hour
Goes well with: rice, green tea
Calories per portion: 280

Steamed lemon ocean perch
Delicious and healthy

What do you need? Either a steamer set or a wide saucepan or wok with a basket and a lid that fits tightly with the basket inside.

Serves 4 hungry people:

1 3/4 pounds ocean perch filets

salt, freshly ground pepper

2 organic lemons

1 bunch parsley

1 pound young leaf spinach

1/2 pound mushrooms

4 tablespoons good olive oil

1 Dry the ocean perch filets and cut into strips about 1 inch wide. Season with a little salt and pepper.

2 Wash the lemons under hot water and dry. Finely grate the zest, then halve the lemons, and squeeze. Wash the parsley and shake dry, very finely chop. Mix with the zest. Pour the lemon juice and 1 cup water into a saucepan.

3 Thoroughly wash the spinach under lots of cold water—if necessary twice. Drain in a colander. Snip off the hard little roots. Coarsely chop the spinach leaves on a large board, using a big knife. Place them in the basket. Clean the mushrooms, remove the stems, thinly slice the caps. Place on top of the spinach leaves.

4 Now put the fish strips on the spinach and sprinkle with the zest mixture. Drizzle with 2 tablespoons olive oil.

5 Place the basket in the saucepan and cover with the lid. Bring the lemon water to a boil and steam the fish and vegetables over a very high heat for about 5 minutes (starting to count when the water is boiling).

6 Transfer onto plates, season to taste with salt and pepper, and drizzle with the remaining olive oil.

Time you need: 45 minutes
Goes well with: potatoes
Calories per portion: 260

Fried striped mullet
Basic and quick

Serves 4 hungry people:

8 small striped mullets (about 5 ounces each)

4 tablespoons butter

2 garlic cloves

salt, freshly ground pepper

2 tablespoons lemon juice

8 – 10 sage leaves

1 Get your mullets cleaned and have the scales removed. At home, wash again under cold running water and pat dry with paper towels.

2 Melt the butter in the biggest skillet you have. Peel and finely chop the garlic. Season the melted butter with salt and pepper, stir in the lemon juice, garlic, and sage leaves.

3 Place the fish in the hot butter mixture and fry over a medium heat for 4–5 minutes. Turn carefully and fry the other side for 5 minutes. Serve the fish in the frying pan.

Time you need: 20 minutes
Goes well with: bread and wine
Calories per portion: 215

Shrimp tails in garlic
Nice tapa

For 4 hungry people as an appetizer:

1 1/2 pounds shrimp tails (i.e. without heads)

2 garlic cloves, 1 bunch parsley

1/2 pound cherry tomatoes

3 tablespoons butter, 1 sprig rosemary

salt, freshly ground pepper

1 Cut the shrimp tails on the belly side (kitchen shears!), and remove the shell. Make a small incision in the back and remove the black vein.

2 Preheat the oven to 400 °F (convection oven 360 °F). Peel the garlic, wash the parsley and shake dry, and chop both. Wash and halve the tomatoes.

3 Melt the butter in a skillet. Sauté the shrimp tails on both sides for 1–2 minutes. Transfer to an ovenproof dish. Mix in the garlic, tomatoes, and onions and place in the oven. Drizzle with the hot butter and bake for another 8 minutes.

Time you need: 30 minutes
Goes well with: French bread, white wine
Calories per portion: 180

Mussels in white wine
Really easy to do, even in large quantities

Serves 4 hungry people:

5 pounds mussels

1 onion

3–4 garlic cloves

1 red chili (fresh or dried)

3 cups dry white wine

1 bay leaf

salt, freshly ground pepper

1 Wash the mussels and scrub with a brush, if necessary—usually they are already pre-cleaned. Discard any open ones.

2 Peel and finely chop the onion and garlic. Cut the fresh chili lengthwise and deseed. Finely slice. (Crumble or chop the dried chili, if using.)

3 In a very large saucepan bring the white wine, onions, chili, and bay leaf to a boil. Season generously with salt and pepper.

4 Add the mussels, cover, and wait for about 10 minutes. At this point most of the mussels will have opened. If necessary,

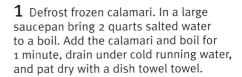

1 Defrost frozen calamari. In a large saucepan bring 2 quarts salted water to a boil. Add the calamari and boil for 1 minute, drain under cold running water, and pat dry with a dish towel towel.

2 With a sharp knife cut the calamari bag into rings 3/4 inch wide. Mix with salt, pepper, lemon juice, and olive oil and leave to marinade briefly or for several hours.

3 Separate the eggs. Whisk the flour into the 2 egg yolks with a pinch of salt, and the mineral water. Leave to stand for about 15 minutes to allow the batter to infuse. Whip the egg-whites until stiff, using a hand-held mixer. Quickly fold them into the batter with a spoon.

4 Heat the oil or clarified butter in a large saucepan (or in a deep-fryer or a wok) until really hot.

5 Coat the calamari rings, one at a time, with the batter and immediately place them in the hot fat.

6 Deep-fry until golden brown, moving the rings about with a wooden spoon. They are done after 2–3 minutes. Take them out with a spatula or slotted spoon and drain them on paper towels. Serve with wedges of lemon and eat immediately while still very hot.

Time you need: 50 minutes
Goes well with: tzatziki or aioli
(pages 90, 136), white bread, salad
Calories per portion: 500

continue to cook for another 2–3 minutes. At this point discard all the mussels that are closed and serve the rest immediately.

5 You do not need any cutlery for eating mussels: Take the mussel or clam out of its shell, and use the empty shell as a tool to remove the next mussels or clams from their shells. At the end of the meal, soak up the juice with pieces of white bread.

Time you need: 25 minutes
Goes well with: white bread, white wine
Calories per portion: 200

Calamari rings in batter
Delicious restaurant food everywhere

Serves 4 hungry people:

1 1/2 pounds fresh or frozen calamari

salt, freshly ground pepper

2 tablespoons lemon juice

2 tablespoons olive oil

2 eggs

1 1/2 cups all-purpose flour

1/2 cup mineral water

about 1 pound clarified butter or 1 pint canola oil for deep-frying

2 lemons

Meat

From hamburgers to lemon chicken. Each to their own...

Hands up all those who never eat hamburgers, chicken wings, chili con carne, hotdogs, shish kebab, duck breast, fondue, roast goose, grilled steaks, goulash, chicken curry, lamb chops, stir-fried turkey, beef olives, saltimbocca, roast pork, breaded veal, meatloaf, or lemon chicken?

If that includes you, then it's OK to get in a huff and just turn to page 133.

For the other 97 percent of you: Please turn the page.

Shoulder or steak?

Roasting takes longer than panfrying because a shoulder of pork is larger than a steak. Sounds logical. But it is not entirely. If you cut a steak from a shoulder of pork, you will have to wait a while before it becomes a piece of tender steak. This is because meat is nothing more than muscle, and when these muscles have had a lot to do in life, as in a shoulder, the fibers are harder and more compacted. Such meat is excellent for roasting and braising. The opposite is true of the meat from the less used areas of an animal: less work makes for thin fibers and tender meat. Since the back is the least used part of an animal, this is where the tenderest pieces of meat for panfrying come from: steaks and escalopes.

Roasting and braising

Beef: For roasting use sirloin tip, rib; for braising and making beef olives use sirloin, brisket, chuck, and round; for stewing use sirloin, shank, short ribs

Veal: For roasting use rump or shoulder; for panbroiling use slices from the loin or round; for stewing use shoulder.

Pork: For roasting, loin, picnic shoulder, rib are best, but any cut can be roasted; for braising use fresh hams or legs of pork.

Lamb: Again, all cuts can be roasted; the leg, shoulder, and breast may be stuffed.

Chicken, turkey, and duck: Roast whole; use the legs for braising. For turkey: the entire breast and thigh can be roasted, the legs braised.

Panbroiling

Beef: Steaks from tenderloin, rib and sirloin; liver

Veal: Steaks from tenderloin, rib and sirloin; scallopini from round and top sirloin; liver

Pork: Steaks and chops from tenderloin, shoulder, center cut; liver

Lamb: Chops from the loin and ribs; Steaks from leg

Chicken, turkey and duck: All the main parts can be quickly panbroiled, although the breasts cook faster than the legs

The steak

Here's what it is
• best beef cuts: filet mignon, T-bone, Porterhouse and top loin strip

• from veal: scallopini, arm or blade steaks
• pork: cut from pork shoulder blade
• lamb: cut from the top of the leg
• from turkey: breast and thigh

Here's what it has
• around 100 calories for turkey, 200 calories for beef, and 400 calories for pork per 3 1/2 ounces
• full of protein—whether this is good or bad is a matter of opinion
• more or less fat; more fat tastes better and signifies a better animal; less fat is better for your health
• lots of vitamin B, plenty of iron and, in fattier pieces, cholesterol

Here's what it wants
• to be cut thickly and evenly
• to be stored in a cool and ventilated place
• not to be placed in a skillet when cold
• to be turned with a spatula or a spoon, not a fork
• not to be tough even when well done
• to be left to stand a few minutes before being served

Here's what it likes
• hot cooking fat
• tangy sauces made from the pan juices
• cold sauces and dips
• a crust from being grilled or broiled
• crunchy side dishes
• fresh salad

Steak to order

Is cooking steak a science? Pros know:
Steaks are usually cooked individually and to order, even at home. Here's how, using an inch-thick sirloin.

Very rare

Panbroil each side for 1 minute. Leave to rest for 2 minutes off the heat. Cook for a further 2–3 minutes, turning frequently. Leave to rest for 2 minutes.

Rare

Panbroil each side for 1 minute. Leave to rest for 2 minutes off the heat. Cook for 3–4 minutes, turning frequently. Leave to rest for 2 minutes.

Medium rare

Panbroil each side for 1 minute. Leave to rest for 2 minutes off the heat. Cook for 4–6 minutes, turning frequently. Leave to rest for 2 minutes.

Medium

Panbroil each side for 1 minute. Leave to rest for 2 minutes off the heat. Cook for 6–8 minutes, turning frequently. Leave to rest for 2 minutes.

Well done

Panbroil each side for 1 minute. Leave to rest for 2 minutes off the heat. Cook for 10 minutes, turning frequently. Leave to rest for 2 minutes.

For a filet mignon

A minute less, for a T-bone steak a minute more. Each additional third of an inch in thickness also adds a minute.

Not sensual enough? Try the five-finger method: Take a finger of your right hand and push against the relaxed surface of your left thumb. This is what a very rare steak should feel like. Now take the index finger of your right hand and push on the palm of your left: rare. Middle finger: medium rare. Ring finger: medium. Little finger: well done. TV cooks swear by this method. Now cooking a steak is all at your fingertips!

Yes, we will

Lots of friends and a big roast • respecting the vegetarians at table • meat from the wok • organic bacon • gourmet hamburgers • turkey legs and not always breast • funky scallops • a little fat • less meat with more taste • often: breaded veal and juicy goulash

No, we won't

A big roast with lots of enemies • putting people off their meat • burgers with additives • meat scallops only from turkey • meat everyday • tooth picks at the table

Let's do the barbecue

Barbecue is what we all do nowadays. Grandpa would have called it "grilling." And he would say: "With all due respect to your low-cal cooking, here we need a little fat." Without fat the meat would be unable to withstand the heat from the coals. Naturally fatty pieces of meat need little help, but lean ones should be brushed with oil or combined with fatty meats: for example with bacon on a skewer. A quality sirloin steak is quickly grilled rare and can therefore be placed over the full heat of the fire without any oil. A pork chop needs a little less heat and a little longer, and so needs a little extra fat added for cooking.

And this is how its done: In order to keep the meat tender and crispy, take it out of the refrigerator 1 hour before cooking. Leave a 1/3 inch of fat around the piece of meat, less if it is well marbled. Then grill at a very hot temperature, continue to cook over medium heat, then leave to rest a few minutes on the edge of the grill. The rule is: The thicker the piece of meat, the longer the cooking time, and the further away it should be cooked from the coals. Around 4 inches for chicken legs, 2 1/3–3 inches for steaks and kebabs. The times are similar to those for panbroiling.

And what kind of a grill? Wood and charcoal can create a romantic atmosphere. But difficulty with getting a fire going, stinging clouds of smoke, and annoyed neighbors can often put a damper on that. This is why more and more people are turning to gas or electric barbecues. Just make sure you have enough space on the griddle, that the gap between the bars is relatively small, and that the heating element is not so badly shaped that you can only produce zebra steaks, half raw, half burned.

Hamburgers...!
...but this is an interesting version!

Serves 4 hungry people:

1 stale roll

2 onions, 2 garlic cloves

1 bunch parsley, 1 tablespoon olive oil

1 pound ground meat (preferably
freshly ground)

2 eggs

1 tablespoon grated zest of
an organic lemon

salt, freshly ground pepper

1 teaspoon sweet paprika

1/2 teaspoon dried marjoram

1 tablespoon strong mustard
or 1 tablespoon ketchup

perhaps some breadcrumbs

3 tablespoons clarified butter

1 Thinly slice the roll, and soak in hot water.
Peel and finely chop the onions and garlic.
Wash the parsley and shake dry, very finely
chop.

2 Heat the oilve oil in a skillet and briefly
sauté the onions, garlic, and half of the
parsley. Remove from the heat and let cool
down a little.

3 Place the meat in a bowl. Squeeze the roll
with your fingers and put it in the bowl with
the meat. Add the eggs and the onion
mixture. Mix and knead well with your
fingers. The more you knead, the less likely
the hamburger is to fall apart. Season to
taste with lemon zest, salt, pepper, paprika,
and marjoram. Knead in the mustard or
ketchup and mix in the rest of the parsley.

4 Divide the meat mixture into small or
bigger portions (from the size of a ping pong
ball to the size of a tennis ball) and roll into
balls (rinse your hands repeatedly under cold

water). If the meat mixture is too soft to roll, mix in a few spoonfuls of breadcrumbs. Press the balls to flatten them and place them side by side.

5 Heat the clarified butter in a large skillet. Fry the hamburgers over a medium heat until crispy, carefully turn, and fry on the other side. This takes about 5–7 minutes each side, depending on the size. Eat immediately —yummy!

Time you need: 1 hour
Goes well with: mustard, freshly grated horseradish, pickles, fried potatoes, beer
Calories per portion: 530

Variations:

Mediterranean meatballs

Combine ground veal with soaked white bread and eggs, lots of freshly chopped garlic, pepper, basil, a few dashes of lemon juice, and 1–2 teaspoons tomato paste. Form smaller balls and only flatten lightly. Fry in olive oil, add 1 teaspoon butter at the end to make them even crispier. Goes well with tomato and pepper salad with scallions, wine vinegar, and olive oil—or a thick and tasty tomato sauce, white bread, and a glass of red wine.

Far Eastern meatballs

Knead ground beef with 1 egg, mix in finely chopped fresh ginger, garlic, and scallions. Season with grated lemon zest, 1/2 teaspoon sambal oelek or another hot chili paste, salt, and pepper. Form small balls and slightly flatten. Cook in gently boiling salted water for 10–15 minutes. To make them crispy, fry for a few minutes in a skillet.

Chili con carne
Ideal party food

Serves 4–6 hungry people:

2–3 onions

3 garlic cloves

2–3 carrots

1 celeriac (1/2 pound)

1 small red, 1 small green bell pepper

1 large can peeled tomatoes (28 ounces approx.)

4 tablespoons oil

1 pound lean ground beef

1 tablespoons fresh thyme leaves

1/2–1 teaspoon sambal oelek

salt, freshly ground pepper

1 can kidney beans (14 ounces approx.)

1 Peel and finely chop the onions and garlic. Wash the carrots and celeriac; wash, halve, and seed the bell peppers. Finely dice everything. Coarsely chop the canned tomatoes.

2 Heat the oil in a large and heavy saucepan. First fry the meat on its own to brown it all over. Then mix in the onions and the garlic, after that the carrots, celeriac, and bell peppers, and at the very end the tomatoes with their juice.

3 Season generously with thyme, sambal oelek, salt, and pepper. Bring to a boil, cover, and simmer over a medium heat for 1–1 1/2 hours.

4 Drain and rinse the canned kidney beans, and add. Continue to simmer for 15 minutes. Season to taste again, making sure the chili con carne is nice and fiery.

Time you need: to be active for 45 minutes, to relax for 1 3/4 hours
Goes well with: bread
Calories per portion (6): 345

Beef olives
Interesting & tasty

For 4 hungry people:

4 thin slices of beef (5–6 ounces each, ask the butcher to flatten them—or do it yourself!)

salt, freshly ground pepper

4 teaspoons strong mustard

8 thin slices bacon

1 large pickle

2 onions, 1 tablespoon flour

1 carrot, 2 celery stalks

4 tablespoons oil

2 tablespoons tomato paste

1/2 cup red wine

1 2/3 cups beef stock or broth

1 pinch cayenne pepper

1 Place the beef slices next to each other and lightly season with salt and pepper. Thinly spread with mustard and cover with 2 slices of bacon. Cut the pickle lengthwise into thin strips and place on the bacon. Peel, halve, and slice 1 onion and also put on the beef olives.

2 To roll the beef slices, first slightly fold the edges of the long sides towards the center, then roll into roulades, starting from a short side. Secure with toothpicks. Dust the beef olives with flour.

3 Peel and finely dice the second onion and the carrot. Trim the celery stalks, removing everything that does not look fresh and crispy. Wash and very finely dice.

4 Choose a Dutch oven or heavy skillet with a tight-fitting lid. Heat the oil and briefly fry the beef olives over a high heat on all sides to brown. Season with salt and pepper, and take out of the pan.

5 Place all the diced vegetables in the pan and sauté over a medium heat. Stir in the tomato paste, pour in the wine, and bring to a boil. Add the stock, and transfer the beef olives back to the pan. Cover and simmer over a gentle heat for about 1 hour.

6 After that hour, you'll find very tender beef olives and a delicious sauce. To further improve the sauce, briefly remove the beef olives again, and reduce the sauce, uncovered, over a high heat, while stirring. Generously season with salt, pepper, and cayenne pepper. Return the beef olives to the sauce and heat.

Time you need: to be active for 45 minutes, to relax for 1 hour
Goes well with: mashed potatoes or pasta
Calories per portion: 500

Spicy chicken wings in lemon
A barbecue favorite

Serves 4 to nibble:

12 chicken wings with lots of meat on

1 sprig fresh rosemary

4–5 tablespoons lemon juice

1 big tablespoon honey

1 tablespoon tomato ketchup

1 teaspoon Worcestershire sauce

1–2 dried red chilies

salt, freshly ground pepper

1 Wash the chicken wings under cold water and thoroughly pat dry with paper towels. Take the needles off the rosemary sprig and very finely chop. In a bowl, combine them with the lemon juice, honey, ketchup, and Worcestershire sauce. Crumble or chop the dried chilies. Season the marinade to taste with salt, pepper, and chilis.

2 Brush each chicken wing with the marinade and place in a bowl. Drizzle with the rest of the marinade, cover, and chill.

3 Grill the chicken wings on the barbecue on both sides until crispy. It'll take about 10 minutes. (If the weather is bad, turn on the oven, put a tray in the bottom of the oven

to collect the fat. Place the chicken wings directly on a rack, baste, and place in the upper part of the oven—don't forget to turn!)

Time you need: 15 minutes plus broiling or oven baking
Goes well with: baked potatoes, salad
Calories per portion: 375

Sweet and sour pork
Let's wok!

Serves 4 hungry people:

1 1/2 pounds lean pork scallops

1 leek

1/2 cucumber

1 piece fresh ginger (as big as your thumb)

3–4 garlic cloves

2 tablespoons sugar

4 tablespoons rice vinegar or white wine vinegar

3–4 tablespoons soy sauce

4 tablespoons sake (or dry sherry)

2 teaspoons cornstarch

1 tablespoons tomato paste

cayenne pepper to taste

6 tablespoons oil

1 Halve the pork scallops lengthwise and then cut into small pieces crosswise.

2 Trim the leek, slice open lengthwise, and thoroughly wash inside and out under running water. Very finely slice. Peel the cucumber, cut in half lengthwise, remove the seeds, and slice. Peel and chop the ginger and the garlic.

3 Now prepare the sauce: With a whisk combine the soy sauce, sake, cornstarch, and tomato paste. Season to taste with cayenne pepper.

4 Pour the oil in the wok and heat over a high heat. First stir-fry the meat strips for 1 minute. Move them to the edge of the wok, and then stir-fry the leek, ginger, and garlic for 1 minute. Stir in the meat and the cucumber, pour in the sauce, and very briefly bring to a boil. Simmer for 1 minute while stirring, until the sauce thickens.

Time you need: 35 minutes
Goes well with: rice
Calories per portion: 350

Mild chicken curry
Asia for beginners

Serves 4 hungry people:

1 piece fresh ginger (as big as your thumb)

1 small onion

2 garlic cloves

1 organic lemon

1 tablespoon curry paste

4 boneless chicken breasts (about

5 ounces each)

2 tablespoons clarified butter

2–3 tablespoons soy sauce

1 can unsweetened coconut milk

(14 ounces approx.)

1 pinch sugar, salt

1 Peel and finely chop the onion, ginger, and garlic. Grate the lemon rind, squeeze the lemon. Mix with the curry paste.

2 Cut the chicken breasts into strips 3/4 inch wide. Heat the clarified butter in a large skillet or wok. Briefly fry the chicken strips on all sides over a high heat; remove from the pan.

3 Discard the fat, just leaving a thin film. Pour in the soy sauce, bring to a boil, and scrape the bottom of the pan. Remove the top cream layer from the coconut milk. Stir in half of it, reserve the rest.

4 Stir in the curry paste, simmer over a gentle heat for 1–2 minutes, while stirring constantly. Season with a pinch of sugar and slowly stir in the coconut milk. Mix in the lemon juice and, at the very end, the remaining coconut milk cream. Return the chicken to the skillet, season with salt, and heat through.

Time you need: 45 minutes
Goes well with: rice
Calories per portion: 310

123

Wiener schnitzel
Has to be veal!

Serves 4 really hungry people:

4 veal scallops (about 6 ounces each)

3 tablespoons flour, 2 eggs

1 cup breadcrumbs

salt, freshly ground pepper

3 tablespoons sunflower oil

1/3 stick butter, 1 lemon

1 Cover the veal scallops with plastic wrap and beat them with a meat mallet or another blunt instrument.

2 Get 3 large soup plates ready. Fill the first with flour, crack the eggs into the second and beat them, and pour the breadcrumbs into the third.

3 Lightly season the scallops with salt and pepper. Turn them in the flour and shake off the excess. Dip them in the beaten eggs and then turn them gently in the breadcrumbs to coat them completely—don't press too hard.

4 Heat the oil in a large skillet and melt the butter. Fry the Wiener schnitzel on one side until golden-brown, then turn them over and fry on the other side. Each side will take

about 2–3 minutes. Cut the lemon into wedges and serve with the schnitzel.

Time you need: 30 minutes
Goes well with: potato and cucumber salad, fried potatoes, or just green salad
Calories per portion: 485

Saltimbocca
Very classy

Serves 4 gourmets:

8 small veal scallopini (1 1/4 pounds)

8 thin small slices prosciutto ham

8 medium sage leaves

3–4 tablespoons butter

salt, freshly ground pepper

1/2 cup dry white wine

1 First beat the little scallopini with a meat mallet. Place 1 slice of ham and 1 sage leaf on each and secure with a toothpick. Melt 2 tablespoons butter in a big skillet and panfry the meat over a gentle heat for 2 minutes on each side. Season with salt and pepper.

2 Remove the meat from the skillet and keep warm (by covering with a lid or foil). Pour in the wine, bring to a boil, and scrape the bottom of the pan with a spatula. The

bits sticking to the pan will add flavor to the sauce. Add the rest of the butter and whisk until it has melted. Return the scallopini to the frying pan and heat. That's it.

Time you need: 25 minutes
Goes well with: Italian dry white wine, Italian bread, peas
Calories per portion: 315

Filet mignon with onions in red wine
Dinner for two

Serves 2 hungry people:

2 small onions

1/2 teaspoon black peppercorns

2 filet mignon (7 ounces each)

2 tablespoons oil

2 tablespoons butter (1 tablespoon cold)

1/2 cup red wine, salt

1 Preheat the oven at the lowest level—the steaks will briefly rest there after panfrying.

2 Peel, halve, and slice the onions. Finely crush the peppercorns in a mortar (if you do not have a pestle and mortar, use coarsely ground pepper).

3 Pat the filets dry with paper towels. Heat the oil in a nonstick skillet over a high heat. Panfry the steaks for about 2 minutes, until they no longer stick to the pan but can be moved with a spatula. Turn the filets—using a spatula (don't use the sharp prongs of a fork!).

4 Add 1 tablespoon butter and cook the filets another 2, 6 or 8 minutes—depending on whether you like them rare, medium, or well done. Transfer to a plate, season with salt and pepper, and place in the oven to rest.

5 Stir the onions into the hot frying fat and sauté. Pour in the red wine and bring to a boil. Stir in the cold butter in little knobs. Slightly season the sauce with salt and pepper and pour it over the filets.

Time you need: 20 minutes
Goes well with: red wine, fried potatoes
Calories per portion: 410

Turkey scallops in a wok
Raid the spice stalls in the (super)market

Serves 4 hungry people:

1 1/2 pounds turkey scallops

1 bunch scallions

3 carrots

1 small red bell pepper

1 piece fresh ginger (roughly as big as your thumb)

2 tablespoons olive oil

1 teaspoon cilantro seeds

1 teaspoon cumin seeds

2 tablespoons lemon juice

1 teaspoon ground turmeric (adds the yellow color)

1/2–1 teaspoon sambal oelek

4 tablespoons cashew nuts or peanuts

2–3 tablespoons sunflower oil

1 Cut the turkey scallops in half lengthwise, then crosswise into thins strips about 3/4 inch wide.

2 Trim the scallions, removing the roots and any green bits which no longer seem to

be fresh. Wash the scallions, halve the bigger ones lengthwise and then cut into pieces about 1 inch long. Peel the carrots and slice.

3 Wash the bell pepper, halve lengthwise, seed and remove the membranes. Coarsely chop the bell pepper. Peel the ginger and cut into a few pieces. Place both in a blender, add olive oil, cilantro and cumin seeds. Purée and mix in the lemon juice and ground turmeric. Season with sambal oelek.

4 Heat the wok without oil. Add the nuts and briefly toast while stirring. Remove from the wok when they start to give off their aroma and certainly before they turn black.

5 Pour some oil in the wok and stir-fry the scallions and carrots for 3–4 minutes. Move to the side, pour another 1–2 tablespoons oil in the middle and stir-fry the turkey strips over a high heat—but only very briefly, not more than 1 minute. Mix with the vegetables on the side of the wok, stir in the pepper sauce, and add a few tablespoons water. Fry for another 2 minutes. Sprinkle with the nuts before serving.

Time you need: 40 minutes
Goes well with: rice—and you must eat with chopsticks!
Calories per portion:325

Hungarian goulash à la Bacsi
The most famous Hungarian export

No, not a spelling error, although it is also Basic. "Bacsi" means friend in Hungarian. And Imre Bacsi, working on a stud farm on the Austro-Hungary border, once cooked a goulash that with its rich taste and silken sheen was a true reminder of the Austro-Hungarian empire—a truly royal experience. Many onions, large pieces of meat, long simmering in its own juices was his secret. Here we share Bacsi's secret with you in all its delicious details.

Serves 4–6 hungry people:

1 1/2 pounds onions

3 garlic cloves

2 1/2 pounds beef (chuck or round steak)

4 tablespoons lard or oil

5 tablespoons sweet paprika

1 teaspoon dried marjoram

1 teaspoon dried thyme

1 teaspoon caraway seeds

1 tablespoon vinegar

salt, freshly ground pepper

1 Start with peeling and dicing the onions and garlic. On the right you can see how a professional does it—but chopping will do the trick too.

2 Now cut the meat—and definitely not into small pieces, they should be at least 1 1/2 inches long and not too thin. Remove all the stringy bits.

3 Heat the fat in a Dutch oven over a medium heat. Sauté the onions until they turn transparent and almost brown—but only almost!

4 Paprika, the first round: add 3 tablespoons to the onions together with the garlic, marjoram, thyme, and caraway seeds and sauté briefly. Then pour in the vinegar and 8–10 tablespoons water.

5 Now, and really only now, add the meat. To give it a chance to brown, don't stir. But it shouldn't really fry in order for it to become really tender.

6 Now season with salt and pepper and stir. Turn down the heat, cover, and simmer. No water? No—no water. The onions and the meat develop their own juices which are sufficient for the goulash to braise for a long time without burning. Only at the very end, when the sauce has been reduced almost completely, you can add a little water. But never a lot, because the meat must not boil or it will become tough.

7 After a good 1 1/2 hours or a little more the meat is practically cooked. Now it is time to add the rest of the paprika and pour in some water after all, enough to barely cover the goulash. After simmering for 15 minutes, it will be perfect. All you need to do now is season to taste.

Time you need: to be active for 1 hour, relax for 1 1/2 hours
Goes well with: boiled potatoes and salad, beer, or red wine
Calories per portion: (6): 390

Basic Tip

If you like it really hot, you can of course make the goulash spicier — even if it is not the original Hungarian way to do so. Simply stir in some rose paprika or cayenne pepper at the end. You may also like to add some vegetables — small pieces of peppers for example or peeled tomatoes or thinly sliced white cabbage. Just mix the vegetable in with the rest before you cover the saucepan to braise the meat.

Sherry chicken
The Spanish version of the French coq au vin

Serves 2–3 hungry people:

1 chicken, cut into 6 pieces (2 legs, 2 wings,
2 breasts)

salt, freshly ground pepper

1 tablespoon sweet paprika

2 onions

1 small red and 1 small yellow or green bell
pepper

2–3 garlic cloves

3 tablespoons oil

1 cup dry sherry

1/2 cup chicken stock

1 Briefly rinse the chicken pieces, and pat
dry with paper towels. Rub in salt, pepper,
and paprika.

2 Peel, halve, and thinly slice the onions.
Wash and halve the bell peppers, seed, and
remove the membranes. Halve the peppers
again and cut into thin strips. Peel and finely
chop the garlic.

3 Heat the oil in a wide, lidded saucepan.
Fry the chicken pieces on all sides over
a medium heat for about 10 minutes until
crispy. Mix in the onions, peppers, and garlic
and briefly sauté.

4 Now pour in the sherry and the stock
and braise the chicken over a gentle heat for
10–12 minutes. Cover, remove from the heat,
and leave to stand for 10 minutes. Done!
Season to taste with salt and lots of freshly
ground pepper.

Time you need: 50 minutes
Goes well with: bread or rice
Calories per portion (3): 770

Roast chicken with lemon stuffing
Beautifully fresh and lemony

Serves 2–3 hungry people:

1 chicken (about 3 pounds)

salt, freshly ground pepper

3 tablespoons olive oil

1 large organic lemon

2–3 sprigs fresh thyme (or 1 sprig fresh
rosemary)

1 Rinse the chicken under cold running
water and pat dry with paper towels. For
now, just season with salt and pepper inside.
Preheat the oven to 430 °F (convection oven
400 °F). Brush an ovenproof dish with
1 tablespoon oil.

2 Wash the lemon under hot water, dry.
Prick the lemon with a fork from top to
bottom and all around (to allow the juice
to run out, making the chicken fresh and
lemony on the inside). Push the lemon inside
the chicken, add the herb sprigs. Cross
the legs and tie together. Now season the
outside of the chicken with salt and pepper
and rub in the rest of the olive oil.

3 Transfer the stuffed chicken to an ovenproof dish, placing it on its side. Put in the oven on the second rack from the bottom and roast for 20 minutes. Then turn the chicken onto its other side and roast for another 20 minutes. Regularly pour the excess roasting fat in the ovenproof dish over the chicken, using a spoon.

4 At the end, turn the chicken on its back (breast facing upwards) and continue to roast and baste for another 25 minutes. Now prick the legs with a small skewer—if the juice still runs reddish, continue to roast. If the juice runs clear, the chicken is cooked and should be served immediately.

Time you need: to be active for 10 minutes, to relax for a good hour, although with some interruptions
Goes well with: salad and bread to mop up
Calories per portion (3): 370

The 180-degree duck breast
Fantastically Basic

Serves 2 hungry people:

2 duck breasts (at least 1 pound in total)

salt, freshly ground pepper

1 Set the oven to 180 °F—check with an oven thermometer.

2 Score the duck's skin and the layer of fat underneath in a diamond pattern (but do not cut into the meat). Rub with pepper and salt.

3 Heat an ovenproof skillet. Place the duck breast skin side down in the pan and brown over a high heat. Turn and briefly brown the other side.

4 Transfer the skillet to the oven—and do absolutely nothing for 30–45 minutes, because at that low temperature the duck breast will very gently cook, but will stay pink and juicy inside.

Time you need: to be active for 10 minutes, to relax for 30–45 minutes
Goes well with: bread, mango chutney (bought or home-made—recipe on page 90)
Calories per portion: 450

Basic Tip

How to cook a duck breast without using an oven

Season with salt and pepper, score the skin in a diamond pattern. Heat a skillet without oil, panfry the duck breasts skin side down for 10 minutes over a medium heat until crispy. Turn and fry on the other side for a maximum of 10 minutes. Wrap the duck breasts in foil and leave for a bit. They'll turn a perfect pink inside.

Roast pork
Bavaria's best

Serves 6–8 hungry people:

3 pounds pork off the bone with rind

(do ask, however, for the 1-pound bone—

it's important for the sauce!)

1/2 teaspoon caraway seeds

3 garlic cloves, 2 tablespoons oil

1 teaspoon sweet paprika

salt, freshly ground pepper

2 onions, 2 carrots, 1 celeriac

1 bay leaf

1 Score the rind in a diamond pattern, using a sharp knife.

2 Chop the caraway seeds, peel and finely chop 1 garlic clove. Combine with the oil and the paprika. Rub the meat with the marinade, wrap in foil, and chill overnight.

3 Preheat the oven to 480 °F (convection oven 425 °F) a good 3 hours before you intend to eat.

4 Unwrap the pork and sprinkle with salt and pepper on all sides. Place in a large roasting pan with the rind facing downwards. Put in the hot oven on the lowest rack to brown. Turn to briefly brown on all the other

sides to seal the juices. Remove the meat, and put the bones into the roasting pan. Then tranfer the meat back into the pan with the rind facing upwards.

5 Leave to roast for 30 minutes, baste with the roasting fat from time to time. Meanwhile, peel and finely dice the onions, carrots, and celeriac. Just peel the rest of the garlic.

6 Reduce the oven to 360 °F (convection oven 325 °F), add all the vegetables and the bay leaf. Pour a bit of water (or beer) over the meat, and now it will take another 1 1/2 hours until the meat is crispy on the outside and tender inside. From time to time pour some of the sauce over the meat and if necessary add some more water or beer.

7 Take the roasting pan out of the oven, turn off the oven, and return the roast back into the oven to rest until the sauce is done. Strain the sauce into a saucepan and reduce a little. Season to taste and serve with the roast pork.

Time you need: 15 minutes the evening before, to be active for 30 minutes the next day, to relax for 3 hours (with a few interruptions)
Goes well with: dumplings
Calories per portion (8): 390

Pot roast
in red wine
Molto italiano,
molto buono

Serves 4–6 hungry people:

2 garlic cloves

2 1/2 pounds beef for a pot roast (ask

your butcher for the best cut!)

2 stalks celery

2 carrots, 1 onion

3 tablespoons olive oil

2–3 tablespoons butter

salt, freshly ground pepper

1 1/2 cups dry red wine

2 cloves, 1 bay leaf

1 small can peeled tomatoes (14 ounces

approx.)

1 cup meat stock

freshly ground nutmeg

1 Peel the garlic and cut into thin slivers. Make little cuts in the meat and push the garlic in.

2 Wash and trim the celery stalks. Peel the carrots and onion. Finely dice all the vegetables.

3 Heat the olive oil in a big roasting pan, add the butter and melt in the hot oil. Brown the meat on all sides to seal it.

4 When the meat has been browned all over, add all the vegetables and sauté in the roasting fat. Season with salt and pepper, pour in the red wine, and bring to a boil over a high heat. Add the cloves and the bay leaf.

5 Coarsely chop the canned tomatoes and mix them together with the tomato juice with the other vegetables in the pan. Now pour in the stock and season with nutmeg, cover—and relax for 3 hours! The pot roast should now be left alone to braise over a low heat—it must not boil.

6 Remove the pot roast from the pan, strain the sauce through a very fine strainer (do not use a pasta colander). But if you prefer the sauce with little vegetable bits floating in it, you do not need to do this. You do, however, need to bring the sauce to a boil again and season it to taste with salt and pepper.

Time you need: to be active for 30 minutes, to relax for 3 hours
Goes well with: polenta (easy to prepare, just follow the instructions on the package), full-bodied Italian red wine
Calories per portion (6): 405

Leg of lamb with a herb crust
Ideal for dinner in winter

Serves 4–6 hungry people:

1 organic lemon

2 pounds boned leg of lamb

2 pounds potatoes (waxy variety)

1 1/2 pounds ripe tomatoes

6 tablespoons olive oil

salt, freshly ground pepper

3 tablespoons clarified butter

1 big bunch parsley

4 garlic cloves

4 tablespoons bread crumbs

1/4 cup freshly grated Pecorino cheese

(or Parmesan)

1 Wash the lemon under hot water, dry, and grate the zest. Halve the lemon and squeeze. Rub the lamb with the lemon juice.

2 Wash, peel, and thinly slice the potatoes. Immerse the tomatoes in a bowl of boiling water for 30 seconds, then cold water for 1 minute, until cool enough to peel off the skins. Dice the tomatoes.

3 Brush a large roasting pan with 2 tablespoons olive oil. Place the potato slices in the dish, season each layer with salt and pepper. Spread 2 tablespoons clarified butter in little knobs evenly on the potatoes. Cover with the diced tomatoes. Preheat the oven to 360 °F (convection oven 325 °F).

4 Wash the parsley, shake dry, and chop as finely as possible. Peel and very finely chop the garlic. Mix the parsley and the garlic with the breadcrumbs and the grated lemon zest. Combine just over half of this mixture with the remaining 4 tablespoons olive oil to make a paste. Mix the rest with the grated cheese.

5 Season the lamb with salt and pepper and coat on all sides with the parsley paste. Place the leg of lamb on top of the potatoes. Roast in the center of the oven for 1 1/4 hours.

6 After that time increase the temperature to 425 °F (convection oven 400 °F). Sprinkle the parsley and cheese mixture over the lamb and the potatoes and spread with the rest of the clarified butter in little knobs. Return to the oven and roast for 10–15 minutes more until crispy.

Time you need: to be active for 45 minutes, to relax for 1 1/2 hours with only 2 minutes interruption
Goes well with: dry Italian red wine
Calories per portion (6): 700

131

Veget

...are (almost) everything that grows and can be eaten after the harvest

ables

...are (almost) everything that grows and can be eaten after the harvest.

...can be the roots, stalks, leaves, fruits, or even seeds of a plant.

...are ancient and originally wild. In China and Egypt the idea emerged, thousands of years ago, to cultivate what was until then only collected. By the time vegetable-growing reached Europe, the Middle Ages were almost over.

...can be tomatoes, lima beans, snap beans, peppers, and potatoes, all native to the Americas. The cucumber comes from India, spinach from the Caucasus.

...can be fried, steamed, cooked, braised, and broiled.

Proof from page 136 onward

What is left after cleaning

How much do you need to buy? Remember that a certain amount will be lost after preparation. And much more will be needed if served as a main course rather than a side dish. Eight examples of what is left from 7 ounces of a vegetable after cleaning.

Snow peas
Top and tail, remove the string—lose 1/3 ounce

Young leaf spinach
Remove the larger stalks and wilted leaves—lose 2/3 ounce

Asparagus
Cut off ends, depending on variety, peel—lose 1 1/2 ounces

Pepper
Remove stalk, seeds and membranes—lose 1 3/4 ounces

Scallions
Remove roots, dark green leaves and wilted leaves—lose 2 ounces

Kohlrabi
Remove long stalk, peel, remove woody parts—lose 2 1/2 ounces

Broccoli
Remove stalk, remove thick stems, remove yellow florets—lose 2 3/4 ounces

Leeks
Remove root end, outer leaves and dark green—lose 3 1/2 ounces

I don't want a corn chicken

Perhaps vegetarians are the most sensual eaters among us. It's great that it is cool not to eat meat. But only greens, won't that make you sick? If your plate is as colorful and varied as the grocery store, you can't go far wrong.

For those who need a little practice, if you still use milk from a cow, you are a lacto-vegetarian. If you include the eggs from a chicken, you are an ovo-lacto-vegetarian. If you eat fish, but no meat, you are a pesco-vegetarian.

Greens, legumes, and nuts are capable of providing the most important elements to be found in eggs and milk. This is why some vegetarians want no animal products at all. Not even honey from the bees. And why they prefer everything raw!

We think the Asian balance is better: one vegetable meal per day, one vegetable day per week, one vegetable week per month. and one vegetable month per year.

Makes seven lives from one.

Quick—something fresh

Tiresome vegetables! Why can't they all be cooked the same way? Well, because they don't taste alike either. For some bite to be left in the vegetable pot, here are the best cooking times for some vegetables.

1 minute
leaf spinach steamed

2 minutes
zucchini and mushroom slices stir-fried, tomatoes steamed

3–4 minutes
leek rings steamed

5 minutes
diced bell peppers steamed

8 minutes
broccoli florets simmered

10–12 minutes
fennel strips steamed, asparagus and cauliflower simmered

12–15 minutes
celery and carrot slices steamed, string beans simmered

15–20 minutes
Brussels sprouts steamed, potatoes simmered

20 minutes
red lentils simmered

45 minutes
brown lentils simmered

Keep fit,gorgeous, smart, & happy

Vegetables are healthy, of course. But that they are specifically good for brain, soul, and complexion is less well known.

	fit	gorgeous	smart	happy
Eggplant	regulates cholesterol	nourishes skin	stimulates thought	relaxes
Beans	boost power; cleanse the body	strengthen hair, skin, bones, and teeth	build strong nerves	activate
Carrots	provide energy; boost vision	make eyes shine; give skin color, protection, and help it regenerate	feed the brain	strengthen
Pepper	reinforces the immune system	firms up skin and nourishes hair	concentrates thought	makes happy; heals wounds
Cabbage	activates muscles and digestion	cleanses the skin; heals wounds	allows thoughts to flow freely	makes merry

Yes, we will

Asparagus in spring, bell peppers in summer, pumpkin in the fall, red cabbage in winter • stir-frying and grilling • carrots as a snack • organic vegetables • creamed vegetables • vegetable curry • ALL THE TIME: vegetable market visits

No, we won't

Asparagus in winter, red cabbage in spring etc. • hours of boiling • vegetables swamped in a roux • only frozen or canned vegetables • intolerance toward meat eaters • NEVER EVER: vegetables as an aside, as in "meat and two veg"

Did you know?

No one can choose their relatives, not even the king asparagus. Botanical families are as mixed up as any. Which of the following are relatives?

a   Savoy cabbage and radish
b   broccoli and arugula
c   cabbage and artichoke
d   potato and sweet potato
e   spinach and beet
f   pearl onions and asparagus
g   turnip and carrot
h   potato and tomato

Answers: all except for d and g

Our favorite vegetable
The tomato

Spanish: tomate; French: tomate; Italian: pomodoro

Here's what it is
• round salad tomatoes with normal (and often too) hard skin
• long plum tomatoes for sauces and soups
• vine tomatoes normally (!) with more flavor
• cherry tomatoes with even more flavor
• beefsteak tomatoes with the most flavor

Here's what it has
• 17 calories per 3 1/2 ounces
• 4g carbohydrates (hence the sweetness)
• almost no protein or fat
• carotene and vitamin C

Here's what it does
• makes you fit to fight everyday illnesses like colds
• reduces tiredness, relaxes
• nourishes hair and skin
• protects men from prostrate trouble

Here's what it wants
• to be stored at room temperature
• to be cut with a serrated knife
• to be seasoned or dressed shortly before being served
• to be heated quickly and gently

Here's what it likes
• olive oil, but also butter—makes them even better for you (fat-soluble vitamins)
• black pepper, curry, juniper berries, basil, oregano, tarragon, cilantro, garlic
• a pinch of sugar

Vegetable platter with aïoli
Garlic fans love it!

Serves 6–8 hungry people in the sun:

For the aïoli (home-made garlic mayonnaise from the south of France):

1 slice white bread without crust

1/4 cup milk

4 medium garlic cloves

1 extra-fresh egg yolk

2/3 cup olive oil

lemon juice

salt, freshly ground pepper

For the vegetable platter:

1 pound potatoes

salt

3–4 eggs

1 pound young string beans

2 small fennel bulbs

4 medium carrots

1/2 small cauliflower (or broccoli)

2–3 tablespoons olive oil

1 bunch celery

1–2 bell peppers (red, green, or yellow)

1 bunch scallions

1 For the aïoli briefly soak the white bread in milk. Squeeze to drain off the milk and place bread in a bowl. Peel the garlic, push through a garlic press, and add. Add the egg yolk and combine to a smooth mixture. Slowly mix in the oil, using a hand-held blender. Season to taste with lemon juice, salt, and pepper.

2 Wash the potatoes, cover with salted water and cook (this takes 25–35 minutes, depending on size). Place the eggs in cold water, bring to a boil, and simmer for about 7–8 minutes. Rinse under cold water.

3 Wash the string beans, trim the ends, removing the string, if necessary. In a saucepan bring 2 quarts salted water to a boil, add the beans, and cook for 8–10 minutes. Drain immediately and briefly rinse under cold water.

4 Wash the fennel bulbs, discard the stems. Cut in quarters or eighths. Peel the carrots, quarter or halve lengthwise. Divide the cauliflower into florets, discard the stems.

5 Heat the olive oil in a large nonstick skillet, add the fennel, carrots, and cauliflower, cover, and sauté over a medium heat for 10–15 minutes, stirring regularly (or cook all the vegetables in a little stock).

6 Wash and trim the celery stalks. Wash and halve the bell peppers, remove the seeds and membranes. Cut into broad strips. Wash and trim the scallions, leaving them as they are.

7 Drain and peel the potatoes. Shell the eggs and cut them in half lengthwise. Arrange nicely on serving plates, together with the vegetables. Spoon the aïoli in small bowls and put on the table for everybody to dip in—because that's what the aïoli is there for!

Time you need: 1 1/4 hours
Goes well with: crusty baguette, fresh light white wine or rosé
Calories per portion (8): 510

Tip for a big party:
Prepare everything in advance (except for the potatoes). To gently reheat, pour over a small amount of hot stock or broth, place on an oven tray, cover with foil, and heat in the oven.

Artichokes with mustard vinaigrette
Dead easy, but quite impressive

Serves 4 connoisseurs as a starter:

4 large artichokes, salt

1–2 tablespoons strong mustard

4–5 tablespoons white wine vinegar

or lemon juice

7–8 tablespoons olive oil or sunflower oil

2 sprigs dill or 1 bunch chives

freshly ground pepper

5 tablespoons white wine vinegar

or lemon juice

7–8 tablespoons olive oil or sunflower oil

2 sprigs dill or 1 bunch chives

freshly ground pepper

1 Wash the artichokes, trim the stems. Cut off the upper third of the leaves, using kitchen shears or a really sharp knife.

2 Stand the artichokes next to each other in a saucepan, add enough water to cover the bottom half of them. Add salt, cover, bring to a boil and simmer over a medium heat for 30–40 minutes, depending on size. To test if they are ready, try to pull out an outer leaf—if it's easy, the artichokes are done.

3 While the artichokes are cooking, prepare the vinaigrette for dipping. Combine the mustard (Dijon mustard tastes best) with the white wine vinegar or lemon juice, and whisk in the oil. Season with salt and pepper. Wash the dill or chives and shake dry, very finely chop, and mix in the vinaigrette.

4 Remove the artichokes from the saucepan, drain upside down, and transfer to plates. Spoon the vinaigrette into four little bowls. Pull one leaf at a time from the artichoke, dip the fleshy end into the vinaigrette and scrape the flesh off with your teeth. When all the outer leaves are finished, you come to a part that is inedible—the choke. Scrape it off to come to the artichoke heart—this is the best part, and you definitely need some vinaigrette to enjoy it fully.

Time you need: 45 minutes
Goes well with: fresh baguette
Calories per portion: 185

Asparagus, green glory
A must in spring!

Serves 4–6 hungry people:

4 1/2 pounds asparagus

salt

1 pinch sugar

1 tablespoon butter + 1 stick butter to melt

2 pounds new potatoes

4 tablespoons balsamic vinegar

freshly ground pepper

6 tablespoons olive oil

1 tablespoon capers

basil leaves

grated lemon zest

1 Peel the asparagus—you need a well-functioning potato peeler (or better still: an asparagus peeler), or this part will be a real pain! Start right underneath the asparagus head and move downwards as you are peeling. Continue to do this all around. Cut off the woody ends of the asparagus, and do so generously to avoid the unpleasant strings that might spoil everything later.

2 Now to cook the asparagus: Place the asparagus spears in a wide saucepan, cover with water, season with salt and a pinch of sugar, add 1 tablespoon butter. Cover and bring to a boil, simmer for 8–10 minutes over a medium heat.

3 Wash the potatoes, place in a saucepan, cover with salted water, and cook. Melt 1 stick butter, keep it hot and runny.

4 Drain the asparagus and place on a serving platter. Prepare the sauce, combining balsamic vinegar, salt, pepper, and olive oil.

Pour the sauce over the warm asparagus and sprinkle the spears with capers, basil leaves, and grated lemon zest.

5 Serve the asparagus with boiled potatoes and hot butter.

Time you need: 1 1/2 hours
Goes well with: dry white wine, for example a German Riesling or a Gewurztraminer from the Alsace
Calories per portion (6): 345

Basic Tips

Traditionally, slices of boiled ham or prosciutto, salmon, or veal steaks are served with asparagus. Slightly more unusual but very nice: Serve with crêpes and hollandaise sauce (recipes on pages 52 and 98).

Asparagus can be stir-fried in a skillet rather than boiled in water. Cut the spears into small pieces, fry in a little olive oil or butter, and season to taste with salt and freshly ground pepper. Sprinkle with a very little lemon juice and fresh herbs or freshly grated Parmesan cheese.

Vegetable bake
A recipe with 1001 variations

Serves 4 serious vegetable fans:

1 1/2 pounds pumpkin (without skin)

1 1/2 pounds potatoes

1 bunch scallions

2 fresh red chilies

2 tablespoons butter

1 1/4 cups milk

1 cup heavy cream

1 egg

5 tablespoons grated Swiss cheese

1 teaspoon dried thyme

freshly grated nutmeg

salt, freshly ground pepper

1 Finely dice or slice the pumpkin. Peel the potatoes and very finely slice. Wash and trim the scallions, halve lengthwise and cut in 1-inch long pieces. Cut the chilies in half, remove the stem and seeds, cut into thin strips.

2 Preheat the oven to 360 °F (convection oven 325 °F). Grease a large ovenproof dish with butter. Combine the milk, the cream, and the egg, mix in the cheese, and season with thyme, nutmeg, salt, and lots of pepper.

3 Arrange the pumpkin, potatoes, and scallions in layers in the ovenproof dish, sprinkle with the chilies. Pour in the egg mixture and place knobs of butter on top. Bake in the center of the oven for about 1 hour. Cover with foil after 40 minutes to prevent from browning excessively (maybe even earlier; check from time to time!).

Time you need: to be active for 30 minutes, to relax for 1 hour
Goes well with: crusty French bread
Calories per portion: 580

Tip
A bake is never difficult: Just mix all your favorite vegetables in any old combination. Clean, wash, and chop the vegetables. Precook vegetables such as carrots, celery, cauliflower, or string beans for a few minutes in boiling salted water, rinse with cold water, drain. Layer in a buttered ovenproof dish, pour over a seasoned egg and milk mixture, and bake. You can add ham, cheese, or salami for extra flavor.

Baked leeks with raisins
Unusual but a very tasty combination!

Serves 4 hungry people or 8 as an appetizer:

2 fat leeks (1 pound)

salt, 3 tablespoons raisins

3 tablespoons dry sherry

2 eggs, 1 cup heavy cream

freshly ground pepper

freshly grated nutmeg

1/2 cup cashew nuts (or other nuts)

2 tablespoons butter

1 teaspoon curry powder

1 Trim the leeks, removing the roots and all the wilted green bits. Cut lengthwise and thoroughly wash under running water. Cut into pieces 3 inches long.

2 In a saucepan bring 1 quart salted water to a boil. Add the leeks and simmer for 3 minutes, rinse under cold water. and drain.

3 Preheat the oven to 400 °F (convection oven 360 °F). Soak the raisins in the sherry, and mix the eggs with the cream. Season with nutmeg, salt, and pepper.

4 Place the leeks side by side in an ovenproof dish, and pour over the egg cream. Place in the center of the oven and bake for 20 minutes.

5 Chop the cashew nuts and toast them in a skillet without oil until they begin to give off their aroma. Add 1 tablespoon butter, melt, and stir in the curry powder. Add the raisins in sherry, and reduce while stirring. Sprinkle over the leeks, top with the remaining butter in little knobs, and bake for 5 minutes.

Time you need: 40 minutes
Calories per portion (8): 200

Stuffed peppers
A real classic

Serves 4 hungry people:

1/2 cup rice, salt

1/2 bunch parsley

1 onion

2 garlic cloves, 2 tablespoons oil

1 big can peeled tomatoes (28 ounces approx.)

freshly ground pepper

3/4 pound ground beef

1 egg, 1 tablespoon strong mustard

1 teaspoon dried oregano, cayenne pepper

4 green bell peppers of the same size

1 Pour the rice and double its volume of water into a saucepan, add salt, and cover. Bring to a boil, simmer for 10 minutes, drain.

2 Wash the parsley, shake dry, and finely chop. Peel and chop the onions and garlic.

3 Heat the oil in a saucepan and sauté half of the onions. Add the tomatoes with their juice and chop in the pan. Season with salt and pepper, cover, and simmer over a gentle heat, stirring occasionally.

4 Combine the ground meat with the rest of the onions, the garlic, parsley, egg, and mustard. Mix in the cold rice, season to taste with salt, pepper, oregano, and cayenne pepper.

5 Wash the bell peppers. Slice off a lid at the stem end, remove the seeds and membranes. Stuff the bell peppers with the meat mixture and replace the lids.

6 Place the stuffed peppers in the tomato sauce, cover, and simmer over a medium heat for 45 minutes.

Time you need: to be active for 30 minutes, cooking time 45 minutes
Calories per portion: 510

Another stuffed vegetable

Stuffed tomatoes
Wash and dry 8 large tomatoes, cut off a lid at the stem end. Remove the seeds and discard. Spoon out the flesh in the middle, chop and place in a bowl. Drain the tomatoes upside down in a colander.
Cut the crusts off 4 medium slices of white bread, dice. Fry in 2 tablespoons olive oil, adding 2 pressed garlic cloves. Preheat the oven to 400 °F (convection oven 360 °F). Dice 1/2 pound feta cheese, mix with 2–3 tablespoons crème fraîche, season with salt and pepper. Add finely chopped thyme or parsley, 1 tablespoon capers, and the fried bread.
Stuff the tomatoes with the mixture, replace the lid, and transfer to a greased ovenproof dish. Spread the chopped tomato flesh around it, season with salt and pepper, sprinkle with 3 tablespoons olive oil. Bake for about 20 minutes. Goes well with a green salad.

141

Stir-fry feast
When you really want to get wokking

Serves 4 hungry people:

1/2 teaspoon dried mushrooms

1 big leek

2 big carrots

1 big red bell pepper

1/2 pound bamboo shoots (canned)

2–4 garlic cloves

1 piece fresh ginger (as big as your thumb)

1–3 dried chilies

4–5 tablespoons soy sauce

2 tablespoons sake

3–4 tablespoons sunflower oil

1 cup fresh bean sprouts (or canned)

salt, freshly ground pepper

1 Apart from the wok itself, the most important thing for this feast is a really large chopping board and a big knife. Otherwise, the chopping gets tedious—and using a wok is about chopping. It's a good idea to get all the bowls and plates ready for the vegetables and the other ingredients.

2 But the first thing is to soak the dried mushrooms: Place them in a bowl and pour boiling water over them.

3 Now we can start: Trim the leek, discarding all the wilted bits. Cut the leeks lengthwise and thoroughly wash under cold running water. Very finely slice the leek.

4 Peel the carrots and cut into matchsticks. Wash and halve the bell pepper, remove the seeds and membranes. Finely slice or dice the bell pepper. Drain the bamboo shoots and cut into fine strips. Place each kind of vegetable in its own bowl.

5 The soaked mushrooms should be ready now. Remove them from the liquid, pour the liquid through a paper coffee filter and reserve for later. Rinse the mushrooms, drain, and remove the stems. Slice the cups.

6 Peel and finely chop the garlic and ginger. Crush the chilies with a mortar and pestle. Mix the soy sauce with the sake. Heat the wok and have all the ingredients ready, next to the wok.

7 Pour the oil in the hot wok and heat. Add the garlic, ginger, and chilies, stir-fry for a few seconds. Add a handful of leek, stir-fry, add the rest of the leek, keep stirring. Now move it the the edge of the wok to make room for more vegetables in the middle. Place a portion of carrots in the middle of the wok and stir-fry, then add the rest of the carrots, mushrooms, bell peppers, bamboo shoots— in whatever order you prefer. Usually, it is best to start with the denser vegetables and finish with the delicate ones, which only need to be fried very briefly, but it is a matter of personal taste. The whole stir-frying process does not take much longer than 5 minutes anyway, because all the ingredients are cut into such small pieces.

8 Drizzle with the soy sauce and sake mixture, add a little of the mushroom liquid, and maybe a little water. Season with salt and pepper and leave for 1 minute. Stir in the bean sprouts at the very end, just to heat them. Don't leave the vegetables to cook for too long; they'll only go soggy. Serve in bowls with chopsticks!

Time you need: 45 minutes
Goes well with: rice
Calories per portion: 180

Mushrooms with curried potatoes
The secret lies in the paste!

Serves 4 hungry people:

2 pounds small potatoes

salt

1 pound fresh shitake mushrooms (or fresh button mushrooms)

2–3 garlic cloves

freshly ground pepper

4 tablespoons olive oil

2 tablespoons lemon juice

3 celery stalks

1 bunch scallions

a few mild red chilies, fresh or pickled

1 bunch parsley

1 tablespoon curry paste (ready-made, it exists in many different varieties—if you've found your favorite one, you'll always come back to it!)

1 Wash and brush the potatoes, place in a saucepan, cover with water, add salt, cover, and bring to a boil. Reduce the heat and cook the potatoes for 15–20 minutes until done.

2 Meanwhile you have plenty of time to prepare the mushrooms—just clean them with paper towels or brush them gently. Don't wash them because they soak up the water and become soggy. Cut off the stems and slice the caps. Peel and finely chop the garlic. Combine the garlic, salt, pepper, 2 tablespoons olive oil, and lemon juice and marinade the mushrooms.

3 Wash and trim the celery stalks, finely slice. Wash and trim the scallions and cut into thin rings. Wash fresh chilies, drain pickled ones, cut into small pieces.

4 When the potatoes are cooked, drain, leave to stand for a moment, and peel while still hot. Wash the parsley and shake dry, and finely chop.

5 Heat the remaining oil in a large skillet or wok. Add the celery and scallions and stir-fry for 1 minute. Move to the side and add, bit by bit, the mushrooms with the marinade, fry, and keep stirring. Add the chilies.

6 Halve or quarter the potatoes and mix in well. Stir in the curry paste and stir-fry everything for another 1–2 minutes. Season to taste with salt and pepper, garnish with parsley.

Time you need: 50 minutes
Calories per portion: 240

Spring vegetables
Puts you in a good mood

Serves 4 people who can't wait for spring:

3/4 pound broccoli, 3 celery stalks

1/2 pound asparagus

1/2 pound snow peas

1 bunch scallions

1 pound small tomatoes, salt

juice of 1 lemon, 2 tablespoons butter

freshly ground pepper

freshly grated nutmeg

2 tablespoons balsamic vinegar

leaves of 1 bunch basil

2 tablespoons freshly grated Parmesan cheese

1 Wash all the vegetables. Trim the broccoli, discarding the woody stems. Divide the broccoli into florets, peel and slice the tender stems.

2 Trim the celery, discard everything that looks limp. Slice the stalks. Remove the woody ends from the asparagus, cut into slices.

3 Trim the snow peas, removing the string. Remove the roots from the scallions as well as all the greenery that appears no longer fresh. Cut off the white part with 1 inch of the green. Finely slice the rest of the greens.

4 Briefly immerse the tomatoes in boiling water, refresh under cold water, peel, and finely dice.

5 In a large saucepan bring 2–3 quarts salted water to a boil, pour in the lemon juice. First place the asparagus in the boiling water, followed by the celery, the broccoli florets, and then the snow peas, each 1 minute after the other. Boil for another 2 minutes. Drain well in a colander, reserving the broth.

6 Melt the butter in a large skillet, add the white scallions and the broccoli stems, and sauté for 2–3 minutes. Add the vegetables, pour in a few tablespoons of the broth, and stir in the tomatoes.

7 Continue to sauté for another 10 minutes over a medium heat. Season to taste with salt, pepper, freshly grated nutmeg, and balsamic vinegar. Sprinkle with the green scallion rings, basil leaves, and Parmesan cheese.

Time you need: 50 minutes
Calories per portion: 155

Ratatouille
Summer, sun, ratatouille...

Serves 4 people in search of the sun:

2 pounds ripe tomatoes

2 eggplants (1 pound in total)

1 pound zucchini

1 red, 1 green, 1 bell yellow pepper

2 fresh or pickled chilies

1/2 pound onions, 3–4 garlic cloves

1/2 cup olive oil, 1 sprig rosemary

salt, freshly ground pepper

1 Briefly immerse the tomatoes in boiling water, then cold water. Peel and halve, remove the seeds. Coarsely chop the tomatoes.

2 Wash the eggplants, cut into 1/3 inch thick slices, then dice. Place in a colander, sprinkle with salt, and leave. Wash and slice the zucchini, halve large slices. Wash, halve and seed the peppers, dice.

3 Cut the chilies lenthwise, remove the stem and the seeds, and chop. Peel and halve the onions, slice. Peel and chop the garlic. Rinse the eggplant dice under cold water and dry with a dish towel.

Savoy cabbage roulades
All' italiana

Serves 4 people fed up with winter:

8 nice savoy cabbage leaves, salt

2 onions, 1 garlic clove

3 tablespoons olive oil

1 pound ground pork

1/4 cup freshly grated Parmesan

4 anchovy filets

10 pitted black or green olives

freshly ground pepper

1 large can peeled tomatoes (28 ounces approx.)

2 tablespoons tomato paste

2 tablespoons balsamic vinegar

4 Heat 3–4 tablespoons oil in a large saucepan. Sauté the onions and garlic over a medium heat until transparent. Then add a small portion at a time, all the vegetables in the following order: first the peppers, then the eggplants, zucchini, chilies. Sauté, adding more oil as you go.

5 Season generously with salt and pepper, add the chopped tomatoes and the rosemary. Cover and simmer for 45 minutes over a medium heat. Season to taste with salt and pepper before serving.

Time you need: 1 1/2 hours
Goes well with: crusty French bread
Calories per portion: 250

Celeriac scallop
Very tasty even without the ham

Serves 4 hungry people in the fall:

1 large celeriac (2 pounds)

juice of 1 lemon

4 slices cooked ham

4 slices medium cheddar

salt, freshly ground pepper

2 tablespoons flour, 1 egg

8 tablespoons breadcrumbs

2–3 tablespoons clarified butter

1 Peel and wash the celeriac. Cut into 8 equally thick slices (dice the end bits).

2 In a saucepan bring 1 quart water to a boil, pour in the lemon juice. Boil the celeriac slices for 5 minutes, rinse under cold water, and pat dry with paper towels.

3 Cover half the celeriac slices with 1 slice of ham and 1 slice of cheese and place the remaining slices of celeriac on top. Season with salt and pepper and coat in flour. Slightly beat the egg in a soup plate and put the breadcrumbs in another plate. Dip the celery scallops in the egg, and then carefully turn them in the breadcrumbs.

4 Heat the clarified butter in a large skillet and fry the scallops over a medium heat for 5 minutes on each side, until golden-brown and crispy. Add the diced bits and fry with the scallops.

Time you need: 45 minutes
Goes well with: salad, tomato sauce, mustard and yoghurt sauce with capers, curry sauce
Calories per portion: 400

1 Boil the savoy cabbage leaves in 1 quart salted water for about 8 minutes. Drain carefully to prevent the leaves from splitting. Rinse under cold water, drain.

2 Peel and finely chop the onions and garlic. Heat 1 tablespoon oil in a skillet and sauté the onions and garlic over a medium heat. Leave to cool, mix with the ground pork and the Parmesan.

3 Finely chop the anchovies and olives, combine with the rest, add the remaining oil, season with pepper and a little salt. Pour the tomatoes with their juice into a saucepan, chop, and heat. Mix in the tomato paste and reduce. Season to taste with salt, pepper, and balsamic vinegar.

4 Place the cabbage leaves flat on a work surface. Divide the filling into 8 longish portions, place on the leaves, fold the edges on the sides and roll into roulades. Place them in the tomato sauce, cover and cook for 30 minutes over a moderate heat.

Time you need: 1 hour
Goes well with: crusty white bread
Calories per portion: 450

Glazed carrots
Simply scrumptious

Serves 4 as a side dish:

1 1/2 pounds carrots

salt

1/2 stick butter

1 teaspoon sugar

2–3 sprigs parsley, or some basil leaves, or mint, or chives

1 Peel and trim the carrots. Depending on size, halve or quarter lengthwise. Now cut crosswises into pieces about 1 inch long.

2 Place in a skillet, cover with water, lightly season with salt. Simmer for 5–10 minutes over a medium heat. The carrots must still be firm to the bite. Carefully discard the liquid, leaving just 1–2 tablespoons in the pan.

3 Dice the butter and mix with the carrots, sprinkle with sugar. Sauté for 5 minutes, while stirring frequently to glaze the carrots evenly. Sprinkle with freshly chopped herbs.

Time you need: 25 minutes
Goes well with: meat, poultry, fish
Calories per portion: 130

Creamed kohlrabi
Eastern European touch

Serves 4 as a side dish:

2 kohlrabi (1 1/2 pounds in total)

2 tablespoons butter

1 tablespoon flour

1 1/2 cups vegetable stock

2/3 cup heavy cream

salt, freshly ground pepper

freshly grated nutmeg

1 Remove the leaves and the stems of the kohlrabi. Wash and finely slice the tender leaves. Peel the kohlrabi, cut into 3/4 inch thick slices and then into sticks.

2 Melt the butter in a wide saucepan over a medium heat, stir in the flour, and let it turn light yellow. Don't let it get too dark. Pour in the stock and the heavy cream, mix well, and season with salt and pepper. Add the kohlrabi, cover, and simmer for 15 minutes over a moderate heat until the kohlrabi is cooked and the sauce has turned creamy. Season to taste with salt, pepper, and nutmeg and sprinkle with the finely chopped leaves.

Time you need: 30 minutes
Goes well with: mashed potatoes
Calories per portion: 130

Fried zucchini
For Mediterranean beginners

Serves 4 as a side dish or an appetizer:

1 pound zucchini

2 garlic cloves

3 tablespoons olive oil

salt, freshly ground pepper

1 tablespoon lemon juice

1 tablespoon balsamic vinegar

1 Wash and slice small zucchini, halve larger ones, and then slice or cut all slices into sticks.

2 Peel and finely chop the garlic. Heat the olive oil in a skillet, add the zucchini and sauté. Add the garlic, turn the zucchini, and continue to fry for another 5 minutes. Season to taste with salt, pepper, lemon juice, and balsamic vinegar.

Time you need: 20 minutes
Goes well with: barbecue dishes, lamb
Calories per portion: 70

Tip:
Tastes very nice with pesto: Mix in 1 teaspoon ready-made pesto at the very end.

Sesame spinach
A childhood trauma
revisited

Serves 4 as a side dish:

2 pounds leaf spinach

3 tablespoons sesame seeds

3 tablespoons olive oil

salt, freshly ground pepper

2 tablespoons lemon juice

1 Trim the spinach, removing the root ends, and wash the leaves thoroughly twice under plenty of cold running water.

2 Heat a really large saucepan, put in the wet spinach leaves, and cover. After a few minutes the leaves will have gone down considerably and you will realize why you bought such huge quantities: It will not seem like a lot now.

3 Let the spinach cool a little, drain, and coarsely chop. Put the saucepan back on the heat and briefly toast the sesame seeds. Pour in the oil and stir in the spinach. Season to taste with salt, pepper, and lemon juice.

Time you need: 35 minutes
Goes well with: meat, poultry
Calories per portion: 105

Lentils with shallots
Not from the can!

Serves 4 as a side dish or appetizer:

1 cup lentils, 1 bay leaf

4–5 shallots (or small onions)

5 tablespoons olive oil, 1/2 cup white wine

3 tablespoons white wine vinegar

1 teaspoon strong mustard

salt, freshly ground pepper

1 pinch sugar, 2 tablespoons chopped chives

1 Place the lentils and the bay leaf in a saucepan, cover with cold water, and cook covered until the lentils are soft (40–60 minutes, depending on variety and age).

2 Peel and finely slice the shallots. Sauté in 2 tablespoons olive oil over a moderate heat, until they turn transparent. Pour in the wine and reduce by half. Remove from the heat.

3 Drain the lentils and mix them well with the shallots. Combine the vinegar with the remaining oil and the mustard, and mix in. Season to taste with salt, pepper, and sugar. Sprinkle with chives.

Time you need: 15 minutes plus cooking
Goes well with: duck breast, poultry
Calories per portion: 260

Snow peas in lemon butter
Quick & good

For 4 as a side dish:

1 pound snow peas

2 tablespoons butter

grated zest of 1 organic lemon

and 1–2 tablespoons juice

salt, freshly ground pepper

1 pinch sugar

1 Wash and drain the snow peas, trim the ends, and remove the string, if necessary.

2 Melt the butter in a skillet and stir in half of the lemon zest. Add the snow peas, sauté in the lemon butter for 8–10 minutes, turning frequently. Don't overdo it; they must stay crunchy. Season to taste with salt, pepper, lemon juice, and a pinch of sugar. Sprinkle with the remaining lemon zest.

Time you need: 20 minutes
Goes well with: fish, veal
Calories per portion: 100

Sweet

Do you have a really sweet tooth or not?

Things

Do the test and find out whether you have a really sweet tooth or not.

1. You are invited out for a meal by a really rather nice person. What will you be drinking?
a freshly squeezed orange juice
b a chilled banana smoothie
c only the very best will do

2. The same really rather nice person cooks you a meal for the first time. As they are about to serve dessert you suddenly remember a prior engagement. What will you do?
a I'll stay, naturally
b I'll go, naturally
c depends on the dessert

3. You are enjoying your first breakfast with the really rather nice person. What would make you happy now?
a fresh croissants with a home-made lemon marmalade
b granola with yogurt and fresh fruit
c peanut butter and more peanut butter

Answer key page 151

Five sweet five-minute sauces

Quick fruit sauce
Purée canned fruit such as peaches, apricots, or pineapple together with a little of their liquid, then flavor with lemon juice and/or a liqueur (you can also do this with fresh berries and confectioner's sugar). Goes with everything that tastes great with fruit.

Quick cherry sauce
1 Drain 1 large jar of cherries in a strainer and catch the juice.
2 Stir together 4 tablespoons juice with 2 tablespoons each instant vanilla pudding and sugar. Bring the remaining juice to a boil, take off the stove, and stir in the powder mixture, then bring back to a boil.
3 Add the cherries and leave to cool. Perfect with custards, ice cream, creamy desserts.

Quick vanilla sauce
1 Whisk together 1/2 cup instant vanilla pudding with 2 cups milk. Use very cold milk or chill in fridge for 1/2 hour for best results.
2 Add cocoa powder to make a chocolate sauce. The vanilla sauce goes well with custards, fruit desserts, chocolate cake.

Quick chocolate sauce
1 Heat 1/2 cup heavy cream and dissolve 1 bar of your favorite chocolate in it.
2 If liked, add brandy, fruit syrup, rum, or instant coffee powder to taste. Goes well with creamy desserts, fruits that taste good with chocolate, and light cakes.

Quick mascarpone sauce
1 Squeeze 1 orange and combine the juice with 1/2 pound mascarpone cheese, 1 tablespoon honey, and a dash of fruit liqueur. Goes well with fruit salad, chocolate ice cream, waffles, pancakes.

150

Yes, we will
strawberries in spring, melon in summer, grapes in fall, papaya in winter • use more than three different varieties of apples • use honey or syrup instead of sugar for a change • sweet things with coconut milk • classic desserts • variations on a theme, e.g. chocolate • beat cream with a whisk • ALWAYS: fresh fruit, ice cream, and chocolate

No, we won't
strawberries in December, grapes in April, rhubarb in the fall • "one apple is like another" • only sweetness instead of flavor • appearance more important than flavor • match a heavy entrée with a rich dessert • a dessert that fills you up on its own • NEVER EVER: skip dessert

How sweet am I?

Answer key to the test on page 149
1a: 1 point, 1b: 3 points, 1c: 2 points
2a: 3 points, 2b: 0 points, 2c: 1 point
3a: 2 points, 3b: 0 points, 3c: 3 points

7-9 points: little sweetie
Dessert for you needs to be somehow cuddly and comforting, soft, and possibly still hot, so you can lazily lie in a corner, lapping it up. You don't need any more than that, before or after. But in the long run, you'd like more cuddles.
Your desserts: crème caramel, chocolate pudding, baked apples, poor knight's bake, griddle cakes with mascarpone, plus Mom's semolina: bring 1 pint milk to a boil, sprinkle in 1/4 cup semolina and simmer for 5 minutes, stirring all the time. Beat 1 egg white with 1 pinch salt and 1 tablespoon sugar until stiff. Quickly beat 1 egg yolk into the cooked semolina, then fold in the beaten egg white.

4-6 points: demanding sweet tooth
Simply sweet is not enough for you. You go for the sophisticated surprises. If you can't have that you might be a bit disparaging. It inspires—and frustrates others. So we'd ask you for forbearance. Basic desserts can be really tasty too.
Your desserts: panna cotta, orange crème, crêpes Suzette, lemon tart, mousse au chocolat, plus caffè alla pappa: put 1 scoop vanilla ice cream into a glass, pour over 1 cup strong hot espresso and 1 dash brandy, sprinkle with chopped coffee beans, and serve immediately—that's how easy something very sophisticated can be.

1-3 points: fruity little number
You do like something sweet—as long as it's healthy, cheerful, fresh, and not too much effort to make. This is why you'd rather bite into a sour apple than stare into the oven for ages. Your sparkling personality carries others away. But do you always have to jump up right after a meal?
Your desserts: red berries, fruit salad (au gratin, if necessary), orange crème, lemon tart (as long as you don't have to make it yourself), plus apple quark: Stir together 250 g low-fat sour cream and 5 tablespoons organic apple sauce, 1 tablespoon honey, and 1 pinch cinnamon. Serve with some Italian almond cookies. Quick to make, refreshing, and comforting all at once.

One of our favorite fruits

The apple
Spanish manzana; French pomme; Italian mela

Here's what it is
• the world's third favorite fruit (after citrus fruits and bananas); in the U.S.A. it ranks second after oranges.
• available all year round, from all corners of the world
• most popular varieties in the U.S.A.: Red Delicious, Golden Delicious, Gala, Fuji and Granny Smith
• some other varieties grown in the U.S.A. include: Akane, Belle de Boskoop, Ben Davis, Braeburn, Breakey, Cortland, Early Harvest, Egremont Russet, Empire, Freyburg, Idared, James Grieve, Jonafree, Jonathan, Lobo, Lodi, Mcintosh, Macoun, Merton Russet, Mother, Northern Spy, Pink Lady, Primevere, Priscilla, Ralls Genet, Red Gravenstein, Red Wealthy, Rhode Island Greening, Roxbury Russet, Spur Winter Banana, Sturmer, Sunset, Twenty Ounce, Vista Bella, Winesap, Winter Banana, Worcester Pearmain, Yellow Newton

Here's what it has
• a medium-size apple has 80 calories
• 38 grams carbohydrate in 1 cup of apple juice
• hardly any protein or fat
• plenty of fiber and pectin
• a good amount of vitamin C, depending on the variety

Here's what it does
• stimulates digestion
• refreshes and helps keep you fit
• yes, "an apple a day keeps the doctor away!"

Here's what it goes with
• butter, yogurt, cream
• nutmeg, vanilla, cinnamon, brown sugar
• almonds, nuts, raisins, lemon
• curry, horseradish, pepper, salt

Here's what it demands
• careful handling; it bruises easily
• not to be stored in the fridge
• not to lie next to potatoes, citrus fruits, or bananas for these will make it ripen—and decay—faster
• to be eaten with its skin on
• once peeled to be used quickly so it won't turn brown
• slow gentle cooking

Panna cotta
Wickedly good!

It's even more wicked with heavy cream (and no milk at all)

For 8 as a dessert highlight:
1 1/3 cups heavy cream
2 1/2 cups milk (or 1 quart heavy cream)
1/2 cup sugar + 4 tablespoons
for the berry compote
2 vanilla beans
8 gelatin leaves
1 pound mixed berries (red currants, strawberries, raspberries, blackberries-whatever is fresh and inexpensive at the moment)

1 Pour the cream and the milk into a saucepan and stir in 1/2 cup sugar. Slice open the vanilla beans lengthwise with a sharp knife, scrape out the seeds (these will be the black specks in the cream) with the tip of the knife, and stir into the cream and milk mixture. Add the empty vanilla beans.

2 Bring everything to a boil over a low heat, leave to simmer gently for 15 minutes. Place the gelatin leaves in a soup bowl and cover with cold water to soften them.

3 Remove the saucepan from the stove; fish out the vanilla beans and leave the cream and milk mixture to cool slightly. Squeeze the gelatin leaves gently by hand and add them to the milk, one by one, until they are dissolved.

4 Pour about 2/3 cup of the cream mixture into each of 8 small molds washed out with cold water (small metal molds or china soufflé dishes). Leave to cool and set in the refrigerator overnight.

5 Rinse the berries, leave them to drain, remove the stems, leaves, and mushy parts. Chop up the strawberries. Warm the berries in a saucepan with 4 tablespoons sugar, cooking them only slightly. (They taste good either warm or cold.)

6 Tip the panna cotta out of the molds. (Loosen them from the molds with a knife that you dip into hot water or briefly place the mold in hot water, or both.) Garnish with the berry compote.

Time you need: 45 minutes, plus cooling
Goes well with: espresso, either before or after
Calories per portion: 290

Crème caramel
Everybody loves it

Serves 5 as a sweet finale:

8 tablespoons sugar

1 pint milk

1 pinch salt

1 vanilla bean

4 eggs

1 Make the caramel syrup first: Melt 4 tablespoons sugar in a small saucepan over a low heat until a very light brown in color, stir in 2 tablespoons of water, and then quickly remove from the stove.

2 Pour the syrup into 6 small ovenproof molds (1/2–2/3 cup of the cream should fit into each); tip the molds from side to side so that the caramel spreads evenly over the bottom.

3 Preheat the oven to 350 °F (later: convection oven 325 °F). Fill a deep baking pan for the oven (the drip pan) with water and place at the bottom of the oven.

4 Place the milk in a saucepan with a pinch of salt and the rest of the sugar and heat slowly. Slice the vanilla beans lengthwise, scrape out the seeds, and add them to the milk together with the beans. Bring to a boil briefly and then quickly remove the saucepan from the stove.

5 Beat the eggs in a bowl. Fish the vanilla beans out of the milk and stir a few spoonfuls of the hot vanilla milk into the eggs. Gradually add the rest of the milk, beating well with an egg beater.

6 Pour the egg and milk mixture into the prepared molds with the caramel. Place in the bain marie (the drip pan) and cook for

about 20 minutes until they are set. Remove the molds and leave to cool. Then place them in the refrigerator to become really cold (preferably overnight).

7 To serve, briefly dip the bottom of the molds into hot water, loosen the filling with a knife warmed under hot running water, and tip onto a plate.

Time you need: actively only 30 minutes, relaxing 20 minutes (plus cooling)
Goes well with: espresso
Calories per portion: 190

Variation:
Crème brulée

With this one the caramel is not at the bottom of the mold; instead it forms a crispy layer on top .

Combine 1 pint heavy cream (or milk), 4 tablespoons sugar with the whisked eggs as described above. Pour into the molds (without the caramel) and cook in a pan of hot water (the bain marie). Leave to cool. Prior to serving, place the molds in a dish of ice-cold water (fill the drip pan from the oven with cold water and ice cubes.) Sprinkle each portion with 1 tablespoon sugar and allow the sugar to form a crust under the broiler or in a very hot oven. Allow to cool (otherwise there is a danger of burnt tongues!) before serving.

153

Chocolate pudding
Tastes like the good old days

Strictly speaking it is called "flummery," but we would rather eat pudding.

For 4 pudding eaters:

1/4 pound chocolate (semi-sweet)

2 egg yolks

4 tablespoons sugar

1 pint milk

1/3 cup cornstarch

1 vanilla bean

1 Break the chocolate into small pieces or grate roughly. Place the egg yolks and sugar in a bowl and beat with a whisk or with the whisk attachment of a hand-held beater for a few minutes until nice and creamy.

2 Take 1/2 cup milk and mix into the cornstarch; pour the rest of the milk into a saucepan. Add the chocolate. Slice the vanilla bean lengthwise, scrape out the seeds and add to the milk together with the beans. Bring everything to a boil over a medium heat, stirring all the time.

3 Add the cornstarch mixture, allow to thicken, and bring to a boil over a medium heat, stirring all the time. Remove the vanilla bean and turn off the heat. Stir in the egg yolk and sugar mixture, but do not allow to boil again!

4 Remove the saucepan from the stove, stir for a while, and then leave to cool slightly.

5 Now rinse out 4 molds or 1 large mold (1 quart capacity) with cold water, fill with the pudding, allow to cool well in the refrigerator (at least 1–2 hours.)

6 To serve, dip the molds in hot water, loosen the edges of the pudding with a knife warmed under hot running water, and tip onto a plate.

Time you need: 50 minutes, plus cooling
Goes well with: vanilla custard sauce or lightly whipped and sweetened cream
Calories per portion: 340

If you want a fluffier pudding, fold in 1 stiffly beaten egg white before filling the molds. This does make the pudding more difficult to tip out, though.

Basic Tip
Vanilla custard sauce

A real Basic made from milk, sugar, vanilla, cornstarch, and eggs. Place 1 pint milk in a saucepan and stir with 1 teaspoon cornstarch, 2 teaspoons sugar, and the scraped out seeds of 1 vanilla pod. Whisk 2 egg yolks (or 1 whole egg) with 3 tablespoons sugar; stir in the milk. Heat and bring almost to a boil (only almost!), stirring all the time. Tastes good warm or cold — and not only with chocolate pudding.

Red berries
Makes anyone go weak at the knees

Serves 8 to tuck into:

1 pound red currants

1/4 pound cherries

1/4 pound raspberries

1/2 pound strawberries

1 1/2 cup red berry juice (red currant or cherry)

3 tablespoons sugar

1 cinnamon stick

1/4 cup cornstarch

1 Wash the red currants and remove from the stalks. Wash the cherries and remove the pits (there is a special gadget for this, but you can also do it with a small, sharp knife.) Don't wash the raspberries, just remove those which are no longer nice and fresh. Wash and hull the strawberries, cut the larger ones into halves or quarters.

2 Place 1 cup juice and 2 tablespoons sugar in a large saucepan, add the cinnamon stick, and bring to a boil. Add the red currants and cherries and simmer for 2–3 minutes.

3 Stir the remaining 1/2 cup juice into the cornstarch, add to the large saucepan, and

bring to a boil, stirring all the time, until the mixture thickens. Now add the strawberries and raspberries; add sugar to taste. Remove from the stove, leave to cool, and then remove the cinnamon stick. Leave to become really cold in the refrigerator.

Time you need: 45 minutes, plus cooling
Goes well with: vanilla custard sauce (recipe page 154) or vanilla ice cream
Calories per portion: 95

Fruit salad au gratin
Leftover magic

For 4–6 as dessert:

2–3 pounds fruit (the leftovers in the fruit bowl or anything that appeals to you at the fruit store—preferably a mixture of colors but no citrus fruit)

4 tablespoons lemon juice

2 eggs, 3 tablespoons sugar

1/2 teaspoon vanilla extract

1/2 teaspoon grated lemon zest

2 tablespoons almond or orange liqueur (e.g. Amaretto, Cointreau)

1 Wash or peel the fruit depending on type, chop into small pieces. Drizzle with lemon juice. Preheat the oven to 400 °F (also now convection oven: 350 °F).

2 Separate the eggs. Combine the egg yolks with the sugar, the vanilla, lemon zest, and liqueur. Beat the egg whites with a hand beater until stiff. Stir into the egg yolk mixture.

3 Place the fruit salad in an ovenproof dish, pour over the fluffy egg mixture, and bake in the oven (in the middle) for 10 minutes.

Time you need: 45 minutes
Goes well with: ladyfingers
Calories per portion: 390

Orange crème
Tastes like more

Serves 6–8:

2 juicy organic oranges

1 organic lemon

6 leaves gelatin

3 egg yolks, 1/2 cup sugar

1 1/3 cups yogurt, 1 cup heavy cream

optionally: white chocolate and grated

orange zest to garnish

1 Wash the oranges and the lemon under hot water; finely grate the zest. Cut in half and squeeze out the juice.

2 Soften the gelatin leaves in cold water. Fill a wide saucepan half full with water and heat without boiling. Now you just need a metal mixing bowl that fits into the saucepan (or just a smaller saucepan). Place the egg yolks in the bowl with the sugar and beat well with a hand beater.

3 Now place the bowl in the saucepan of hot water, add the grated zest and juice from the oranges and lemons, and stir until the mixture becomes fluffy and light. Quickly remove from the heat.

4 Squeeze out the gelatin leaves, stir into the cream mixture one at a time and stir until

they have dissolved. Allow to cool briefly. Add the yogurt. Leave to cool for 5–10 minutes.

5 Stiffly beat the cream with a (clean) whisk. Now place the cream in 6 or 8 small molds or in one large mold; place in the refrigerator to set and become really cold. If you like, garnish with grated white chocolate and grated orange zest.

Time you need: 45 minutes, plus cooling
Goes well with: ladyfingers, cookies
Calories per portion (8): 440

Baked apples
From grandma's cookbook

For 4 or even 8—depending on appetite:

2 tablespoons raisins

1/2 cup cider or apple juice

8 small, firm, tart apples (e.g. Granny Smith)

2 tablespoons lemon juice

2 tablespoons butter

2/3 cup flaked almonds

1–2 tablespoons honey

1/4 teaspoon cinnamon

1–2 teaspoons grated zest of an organic lemon

1 Soften the raisins in the cider or apple juice. Preheat the oven to 360 °F (also now: convection oven 325 °F).

2 Wash the apples well and rub dry. Remove all of the cores with a knife without cutting up the apple. Sprinkle the cavities with lemon juice.

3 Grease an ovenproof dish with 1 teaspoon butter. Drain the raisins and pour the cider or apple juice into the dish. Roughly chop the flaked almonds; add the remaining butter, raisins, and honey and season with cinnamon and grated lemon zest.

4 Place the cored apples in the dish and fill the apples with the mixture. Bake in the oven (middle) for about 20 minutes.

Time you need: 45 minutes
Goes well with: vanilla ice cream or vanilla custard sauce (recipe page 154)
Calories per portion (8): 120

Griddle cakes
with mascarpone
Forget the diet

Serves 3–4 as a brunch dessert:

4 eggs

1 pinch salt

1/4 cup sugar

1 tablespoon grated zest of an organic lemon

4 tablespoons milk

1 cup cake flour

1/2 pound mascarpone (or else cream
cheese (not reduced fat) + 2 tablespoons
heavy cream)

2 tablespoons butter

confectioner's sugar for dusting

1 Separate two of the eggs. Place the 2 egg
yolks in a mixing bowl then add the two
whole eggs. Whisk together with a pinch of
salt and the lemon zest.

2 Gradually stir in the milk, flour, and
mascarpone. Beat the 2 egg whites with a
hand beater until stiff. Fold into the mixture
loosely—it should not be an even cream,
the lumps of egg white should be clearly
visible in the batter.

3 Melt the butter in a large skillet (not a
nonstick one) over a medium heat. Pour the
batter into the skillet about 3/4–1 inch thick
and spread evenly. Cook until you can draw
two forks through the batter cutting it into
pieces.

4 Put the forks aside and cook the pieces
of batter over a high heat until they become
crispy all over, stirring and turning them all
the time. Dust with confectioner's sugar and
serve immediately!

Time you need: 35 minutes
Goes well with: applesauce (use ready-
made—or simply cook pieces of peeled
apple covered with lemon juice and water
until soft; season with sugar and cinnamon),
berry compote (see panna cotta page 152),
or any kind of fruit compote.
Calories per portion (4): 555

Blueberry
muffins
Always popular

Makes 12:

1 muffin pan and 12 or 24 paper cases

2 1/2 cups all-purpose flour

3 teaspoons baking powder

1/2 pound fresh or frozen blueberries

1 large egg

3/4 cup sugar

1 teaspoon vanilla extract

8 tablespoons sunflower oil

2/3 cup buttermilk (you can also use milk,

yogurt, or sour cream)

1 Place baking cups in the muffin pan.
If you do not have a muffin pan, use two
baking cups inside each other and place
them on a cookie sheet. Preheat the oven to
360 °F (also now: convection oven 325°F).

2 Combine the flour with the baking
powder. Pour the blueberries into a strainer
and leave to drain well (drink any of the
blueberry juice or keep it for later—you don't
need it for the recipe).

3 Beat the egg in a mixing bowl. Then add
the sugar, vanilla, oil, and buttermilk, mixing

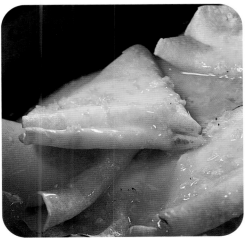

well together. Gradually fold in the flour and then the drained blueberries.

4 Place the dough in the 12 baking cups and bake in the oven (middle) for 20–25 minutes. Turn off the oven and leave the muffins to stand for a moment. Remove from the pan and serve warm or once they have cooled.

Time you need: active cooking 20 minutes, relaxing 20-25 minutes
Goes well with: vanilla custard sauce (recipe page 154)
Calories per muffin: 210

Crêpes Suzette
Paper-thin griddle cakes — the elegant version

For 4 Francophiles:

1/2 stick butter for the batter + 1 teaspoon

for the orange sauce

2 eggs

2/3 cup milk

1 pinch salt

2 tablespoons sugar

1 cup cake flour

4 oranges (at least 1 organic)

1 teaspoon vanilla extract

2 tablespoons orange liqueur (Grand

Marnier, Cointreau)

1/4 cup ghee

confectioner's sugar

1 Melt the butter for the batter in a small saucepan and then remove from the stove. Beat the eggs with the milk, season with salt and 1 tablespoon sugar. Gradually add the flour in spoonfuls and mix everything into a smooth batter without lumps.

2 Squeeze 1/2 orange and stir the juice into the melted butter. Stir into the batter; leave to cool in the refrigerator for 30 minutes.

3 Squeeze the other half of the orange as well as 1 further orange. Wash the organic orange under hot water, dry, and grate the zest. Peel the 2 oranges so that you reach the fruit underneath. Cut out the individual segments from between the membranes using a sharp knife. Add the juice which is produced while doing this to the other juice.

4 Now its time for the orange sauce:
Melt 1 teaspoon of butter in a skillet. Stir in the vanilla and remaining tablespoon sugar, brown slightly over a medium heat, add the juice and liqueur and allow to boil for 3–5 minutes until syrupy.

5 Grease a nonstick skillet with ghee and heat. Place a small ladle full of batter in the skillet, tip the skillet so that batter spreads evenly. Cook over a medium heat for 30 seconds to 1 minute, then turn over and cook for a further 30 seconds to 1 minute. Fold the crêpe in half and place in the orange sauce.

6 Cook all of the crêpes, fold them and place in the sauce (grease the skillet with more ghee in between). Dust with icing sugar and serve immediately.

Time you need: 1 hour 15 minutes
Goes well with: for those with a very sweet tooth 1 scoop vanilla ice cream
Calories per portion: 470

Poor knight's bake
Very impressive

For 3–4 to eat their fill,

for 6–8 for dessert:

6 tablespoons butter, 1/4 cup raisins

6 stale rolls (from the day before, or white

bread or brioches)

6 tablespoons sugar

4 medium, firm, tart apples (e.g. Granny

Smith)

1 organic lemon

1 pint milk

3 eggs, 1 pinch salt

1 teaspoon vanilla extract

1/2 teaspoon cinnamon

2 tablespoons pine nuts

1 Preheat the oven to 400 °F (later:
convection oven 360 °F). Grease a large
baking dish with 1 tablespoon butter.
Wash and dry the raisins.

2 Thinly slice the rolls. Melt 3 tablespoons
butter with 2 tablespoons sugar, stirring all
the time. Spread over the sliced rolls and
bake them on a cookie sheet in the oven
for 6 minutes. Cut the apples into quarters,
peel, and remove the cores. Slice the apples.
Layer the apple pieces and the sliced rolls
in the baking dish.

3 Wash the lemons under hot water, dry
and finely grate the zest. Whisk the milk with
the lemon zest, the eggs, salt, vanilla, and
the remaining sugar.

4 Pour over the apples and bread; sprinkle
with raisins and cinnamon. Bake in the oven
(middle) for 30 minutes. Then sprinkle with
the pine nuts, place the rest of the butter in
small pieces on the surface, and bake for a
further 10–15 minutes.

Time you need: active cooking 30 minutes,
relaxing 40–45 minutes
Calories per portion (8): 265

Lemon tart
A Mediterranean Basic

A-makes-you-want-more-recipe!

Serves 8–10 foodies:

For the pastry:

2 cups flour

1/3 cup sugar

1 stick cold butter

1/2 organic lemon

1 teaspoon vanilla extract

1 egg yolk

plus dried beans or peas and baking

parchment for baking blind

For the filling:

2 1/2 organic lemons

4 eggs

1 egg yolk

2 cups sugar

1/2 cup heavy cream

1 tablespoon confectioner's sugar

1 Place the flour in a bowl with the sugar. Cut the butter into small pieces. Finely grate the lemon zest, add to the flour with the butter, vanilla, and egg yolk.

2 Wash your hands under cold water so that the dough remains cool. Then knead everything together just until you can't see the small pieces of butter in the dough anymore. Roll the dough out into a circle —

works best if you do this between two layers of plastic wrap. Cut out a pie shape 12 inches in diameter and leave the shell to cool in a pie dish for 1 hour.

3 Preheat the oven to 360 °F (also now: convection oven 325 °F).

4 Cover the dough in the dish with a piece of baking parchment and weigh down with beans or peas. Prebake the dough in the oven (middle) for about 10 minutes.

5 For the filling wash the lemons and grate the zest. Squeeze the lemons. Beat the eggs, egg yolk, and the sugar with a hand beater until very light and fluffy. Add the lemon zest and juice to the egg mixture. Beat the cream until stiff and fold into the egg mixture.

6 Remove the beans and peas and the paper from the prebaked shell. Pour the lemon cream into the pastry shell and bake at 300 °F (convection oven only 250 °F) for 50 minutes until the cream is set.

7 Allow the tart to cool completely. Before serving, turn on the broiler. Dust the tart with confectioner's sugar and brown under the hot broiler. Caution: This doesn't take more than about a minute!

Time you need: active cooking 35 minutes, relaxing 1 hour 45 minutes
Goes well with: espresso
Calories per portion (10): 340

Mousse au chocolat
Always a winner

For 4 serious eaters:

1/2 pound semi-sweet baking chocolate

1/2 stick butter

5 very fresh eggs

salt

2 tablespoons sugar

1 Another recipe with a bain marie:
Fill a large saucepan half full with water and heat. Place a metal bowl of the right size in the water. Finely chop the chocolate and place in the bowl. Melt slowly over the warm water and over a medium heat only so that the chocolate does not become grainy. Stir occasionally.

2 Melt the butter in a saucepan and then leave to become lukewarm but still liquid. Stir into the melted chocolate and remove from the stove. Keep the bain marie with the hot water for the egg cream.

3 Separate the eggs. Beat the egg whites with 1 pinch salt until stiff (using a hand beater.) Place the egg yolks in a mixing bowl with the sugar. Place the bowl in a saucepan full of ice cold water (for a change!) and beat the mixture until light and foamy. Then change over to the warm bain marie and beat the mixture until thick and creamy.

4 The Grande Finale: Combine the egg mixture with the chocolate mixture. Then stir in a third of the beaten egg whites. Now fold (don't mix) in the rest of the egg whites very loosely so that they stay light and fluffy. Place the mousse in bowls and cool thoroughly (at least 3 hours in the refrigerator.)

Time you need: 30–40 minutes (depending on practice and experience with bain maries), plus cooling time
Calories per portion: 535

The not-so-Basic encyclopedia

Did you notice that, up until now, we have written little about blanching or poaching? That's because we wanted to write in a way that everyone could understand.

Admittedly, it is not particularly cool to do so, but we thought it so relaxing to write about food and avoid the usual jargon. It felt like drinking fresh spring water after indulging oneself in Chardonnay, Long Island tea, and latte macchiato every night—and at the same time not to write a literary essay about it, just a cookbook. But why is this book called *Basic Cooking*? Well, do we really need to give a specific reason? Anyway, we seem to have understood each other— or would you be reading the last page if we hadn't? And here's where you find our little encyclopedia. Here you find what you didn't find in *Basic Cooking*—just in case you'll read other cookbooks and need to understand them. But that's not all: We have included what happens after cooking, while eating and drinking—and enjoying smalltalk (see under S).

Alcohol
Can refine—or destroy—a dish or a whole party. In order to avoid destruction, save on quantity not quality.

Apéritif
A gentle introductory drink, which relaxes and awakens expectations. Prosecco, sparkling wine, or champagne are good, so are the wine which will later be served with the meal, beer, or not-too-sweet fruit juices.

Spirits are not good. Typical mistake: "And now a little apéritif to finish off the meal."

Baking
A theme of its own, and rarely the forte of an ardent cook. This is why it hardly appears in this book (although it will appear elsewhere).

Blanching
Placing something in boiling water in order to precook it. Sometimes then rinsed in cold water in order to "freeze in" its color.

Cappuccino
Espresso with lots of hot frothy milk. Cocoa and little cookies are not necessarily required. Also good with whipped cream, but be ready for a scolding from Italian purists. Recommended retort: "You never heard of Viennese cappuccino?" Also in response to the criticism that cappuccino should only be drunk in the mornings, as in Italy: "It's your fault if you get up so early."

Carving
Cutting a roast or a roast bird into portions. Looks good at table if you can do it. If not, food, table, clothes, guests, and the evening are in danger.

Cutlery
Usually helpful. Knife (right) and fork (left) make up the basic equipment; spoon, when needed, to the right of the knife. For meals with multiple courses, work from outside in. Up and coming: chop sticks (placed to the right of the plate, or horizontally in front of it). See also: hands.

Diet
We propose the seven-day Basic diet: For one week, eat whatever you like, but never the same thing twice.

Dousing
The pouring of liquid into the skillet after frying, in order to dissolve the oils and make them into a sauce. Impressive: Let a generous amount of red wine fizz in the pan, especially when the guests are in the kitchen. Dumb: dropping the bottle in afterwards because you are so excited.

Glasses
It is true that a glass makes a drink taste the way it does (for those who doubt, try drinking coffee out of a thin and then a thick cup). The rule is: The more delicate the drink, the more delicate the difference. Champagne is better from a long flute than from a shallow goblet. Prosecco, however, can be drunk from normal white wine glasses. Also important: glasses to the right of the plate; don't forget water glasses; never fill a wine glass more than half full.

Glazing
1. Roast (for example pork) which has had the cooking juices poured over it repeatedly during cooking, and so has obtained a shiny crust.
2. Vegetables cooked with fat, liquid, and a little sugar, so that they are covered with a coat of shiny syrup.

Gossip
"God, what a terrible evening. As soon as someone left, everyone else started bad-mouthing him." "So why did you leave last?" "To avoid that happening to me." A little gossip can spice up a meal. A lot makes it inedible. See also: Smalltalk.

Gratin
Baked dish topped with grated cheese. A gratin is put under the broiler, a bake not necessarily.

Hands and fingers

Ideal tools for kneading, salad mixing (not at table), tasting (only when no one is watching) and greeting guests (after washing). Eating with your hands makes some things easier (sandwich, chicken leg) and lots of things more sensual (asparagus, mussels, strawberries). Sensible: always keep one hand clean.

Manners

If you know how to use them, they will do no harm. Always good: please, thank you, sorry (in moderation). Not so good: over-politeness at informal or unplanned events (it gets in the way). Never good: talking loudly, sneezing, burping and so on.

Marinating

Placing something in a spiced liquid or cream: for example salad or barbecue meat. See also: stewing.

Menu

Looks good and makes guests feel more important. A salad for an appetizer and a dessert turn a meal into a menu. First rule: Don't overdo it. No six-course meals when friends want a quick bite before going to the movies. And don't disapppear for half an hour's swearing in the kitchen inbetween courses because this will kill any conversation. Second rule: Variety! Cream soup, turkey scallops with cream sauce, and dessert with whipped cream is not varied.

Mom's cooking

A conversation enlivener or killer: "Great roast. The last time I had one this good was at my mom's." Great if the cook has no age problems and the other guests add their own memories. Fatal if the person's partner and usual roast cooker is at the same table.

Napkins

Are even useful for the midnight ham sandwich session, as long as they are not artistically folded swans which kill spontaneity and leave you wondering about how long someone has had them in their hands.

Perfume

The tongue can only distinguish the basic flavor of a meal, the subtleties are sensed by the nose. If everyone at table agrees that the overwhelming flavor is musk, violet, or eau de cologne, someone has obviously overdone the perfume. Even worse: scented candles or incense. See also: smoking.

Poaching

Cooking something gently in simmering water. See also: simmering.

Sautéing

Lightly frying, without browning; mostly used for onions and garlic.

Simmering

A liquid simmers when it is just about to boil and small bubbles begin to rise.

Slurping

Wine lovers and espresso drinkers know that slurping can make a good drink better since this enhances the aroma. And the slurping of soup can, in small circles, be seen as a compliment to the cook. Yet: In case of doubt, a good spoken compliment is more appropriate.

Smalltalk

Great for an apéritif, but pretty boring as conversation during the meal. Good themes: weather, television, sports, entertainment, food, drink. Bad themes: natural disasters, the Bible, illnesses, politics, digestion, drinking stories. See also: Mom's cooking.

Smoking

Difficult. But basically simple: Smoking and savoring a flavor don't go together. This is why smoking at table should only take place if absolutely everyone present is a smoker.

Stewing/infusing

1. Cooking—for example: leaving small pieces of meat and/or vegetables to cook in lightly simmering liquid.
2. Infusing—for example: leaving a pasta salad to stand until all the flavors have become thoroughly absorbed and mixed.

Stock

Thick, strong liquid, which is normally cooked from meat bones, fish bones, or vegetables. Good base for sauces and soups. Can be bought ready-made.

Stuffing

Finely ground mixture made of meat, fish, or vegetables, used for—well, stuffing.

Index

164

167